Lessons and Conclusions From the History of Navy and Military Doctrinal Development

Dr. James J. Tritten
Naval Doctrine Command
Foreword by Jellicoe [AI]
Enhanced by Nimble Books AI

Nimble Books LLC

Publishing Information

(c) 2023 Nimble Books LLC
ISBN: 9781608881413

AI Lab for Book-Lovers No. 16
Using AI to make books richer, more diverse, and more surprising.

Algorithmically Generated Keywords

DOCTRINE COMMAND Norfolk; CENTRALIZED MILITARY DOCTRINE; multinational navy doctrine; multi-Service naval doctrine; Naval War College; DOCTRINE NAVY DOCTRINE; formal written doctrine; Imperial Japanese Navy; Naval Institute Proceedings; World War; German Army doctrine; French Army doctrine; Royal Navy; SUCCESSFUL NAVY DOCTRINE; Military Doctrine Development; DOCTRINE MILITARY DOCTRINE; Doctrine Joint doctrine; Naval Warfare; GILBERT STREET NORFOLK; warfare doctrine; American naval doctrine; French Navy doctrine; naval Services; NAVY FORCES; Force Doctrine Center; ORGANIZATION NAVAL DOCTRINE

FOREWORD

In 1995, the end of the Cold War found the US Navy grappling with its role and its future. Dr. James Tritten ably articulated the value of naval doctrine in this historical survey for the Naval Doctrine Command. In subsequent decades, the Navy's doctrine evolved in response to changing circumstances, in some instances successfully, in some instances not. The Navy abandoned long-distance strike aircraft in a doctrinal pursuit of sorties-to-shore, wasted decades on a Littoral Combat Ship that was almost literally all doctrine, and saw its seakeeping readiness degrade at a level even more fundamental than the doctrinal. Today, the US Navy is faced with a peer competitor that can outbuild it. Getting doctrine right has never been more critical.

--Jellicoe [AI]

ABSTRACTS

AUTHOR'S ABSTRACT

There are some excellent lessons to be learned concerning the development of military doctrine by navies in the world. These lessons include:

- Navy doctrine has existed in the past [it is not new];
- It is proper to study the doctrinal lessons of other nations and other services; important doctrinal lessons can be drawn from history;
- Formal navy doctrine suffered a setback with the introduction of new technologies and the end of the Anglo-Franco wars in the Nineteenth Century;
- Pre-war military doctrine cannot forseee all eventualities;
- Centralized military doctrine should not be cast in stone;
- Military doctrine has changed due to a variety of circumstances;
- It is not easy to institute a significant doctrinal change in large organizations; it appears easier to change military doctrine when it is written;
- Measures of effectiveness are needed for military doctrine;
- Successful navy doctrine has been prepared by a variety of individuals;
- Doctrine must be meaningful;
- Joint and multinational doctrine become more important as national forces downsize;
- Multinational doctrine for navy forces will be inherently different than multinational doctrine for land forces;
- There is no one correct military doctrine;
- There is a doctrinal renaissance in progress;
- Good military doctrine is of no value without good men and women who are trained and provided the proper equipment;
- And naval doctrine is not risk free.

SCIENTIFIC STYLE[1]

Naval doctrine is a complex and ever-evolving field that is influenced by the work of Sun Tzu and Delbruck. It is made up of pre-war, centralized, joint, and multinational elements that are subject to change through air mail sent by liaison officers from various countries to recipients in the US, UK, Australia, and Italy. This study provides an overview of the structure and evolution of naval doctrine within this context.

TL;DR (ONE WORD)

Doctrine.

TL;DR (VANILLA)

Naval doctrine is a set of pre-war, centralized, joint, and multinational principles influenced by surprising figures such as Sun Tzu and Delbruck that can be changed through multinational collaboration.

EXPLAIN IT TO ME LIKE I'M FIVE YEARS OLD

Naval doctrine is a set of rules that all countries with a navy use to work together. It helps them know what to do when they are in a war, so they can work together to win. The rules are written by very smart people and are based on advice from people like Sun Tzu and Delbruck. Different countries talk to each other about the rules by sending letters and messages through special people called liaison officers. The countries that talk and share rules are the United States, NATO, and traditional maritime powers such as Japan.

---

[1] This and subsequent abstracts are machine-generated and unsupervised; use with caution.

ACTION ITEMS

Develop a centralized system of naval doctrine that can be shared among various countries.

Establish a joint committee to review and update naval doctrine on a regular basis.

Utilize a wide range of theories to inform naval doctrine.

Establish liaison positions focused on doctrine.

Viewpoints

These perspectives increase the reader's exposure to viewpoint diversity.

Formal Dissent

The concept of naval doctrine is often seen by some as outdated and too rigid for modern warfare. This view holds that naval forces are now required to act more flexibly and independently, without reliance on pre-determined strategies or doctrines. Furthermore, the traditional notions of joint, multinational operations may not be as applicable in today's world as they once were. Additionally, the reliance on historical figures such as Sun Tzu and Delbrck can lead to a lack of consideration for advancements in technology and other factors that have changed in the intervening centuries.

Red Team Critique

This document does not properly address the need for rapid communication and decision-making in naval doctrine. While traditional air mail is useful for pre-war planning, the reliance on it for post-war situational awareness can lead to miscommunication and delays in decisions being made. Additionally, the scope of this document only looks at naval doctrine through Sun Tzu and Delbruck and fails to look at more recent developments in the field, limiting its applicability to current operational needs. Finally, there is no criteria established as to who should receive these liaison officer's updates; there should be a clear chain of command that is well-defined in order to ensure the proper dissemination of information and to prevent any command and control issues.

MAGA Perspective

The very mention of Sun Tzu and Delbruck in the description of naval doctrine raises alarm bells. The traditional, American way of war must not be replaced by those from foreign countries!

This document is a recipe for disaster, propagating a dangerous system of pre-war preparations, joint actions, and multinational influence. It puts the United States at risk of being outmaneuvered and overpowered on the international front.

In addition, the fact that messages can be sent via air mail is appalling. This means that any foreign country, whose ideas are found to be suitable, can make changes and adjustments to our naval doctrine without permission or even knowledge of the United States government!

Furthermore, this document gives permission to send liaison officers from various countries all around the world to recipients in specific countries such as the U.S., UK, Australia, and Italy. This could potentially open up pathways for those countries to share information and resources, which puts us at a huge disadvantage when it comes to global politics.

Overall, it is clear that the tenets of this document run counter to MAGA ideals and threaten the security of the United States. We must take action immediately to ensure these procedures cannot be implemented and that our traditional principles of war remain intact.

SUMMARIES

METHODS

Extractive summaries and synopsis fed into recursive, abstractive summarizing prompt to large language model.

Reduced word count from 22379 to 40 words by extracting the 20 most significant sentences, then looping through that collection in chunks of 2500 tokens for 3 rounds until the number of words in the remaining text fits between the target floor and ceiling. Results are arranged in descending order from initial, largest collection of summaries to final, smallest collection.

Machine-generated and unsupervised; use with caution.

RECURSIVE SUMMARY ROUND 0

Navy and military doctrinal development lessons from history include pre-war doctrine cannot foresee all eventualities, centralized doctrine should not be set in stone, and that doctrine has changed due to a variety of factors.

It is difficult to make significant doctrinal changes in large organizations; measures of effectiveness are needed for military doctrine; successful naval doctrine is prepared by a variety of individuals; joint and multinational doctrine become more important as national forces downsize; there is no one correct military doctrine; good military doctrine is useless without good people and proper equipment; and naval doctrine is not risk-free.

Written Navy doctrine exists in the form of Naval Warfare Publications (NWP), Strategic Concepts of the U.S. Navy, and doctrinal documents of other navies. Doctrine must be prepared to change during a war and welcome recommendations for change. It is a common cultural perspective on how the Naval Services think about and act during war and military operations other than war.

Introduction of aircraft carriers into the Royal Navy and Sun Tzu's influence on the Japanese Imperial Navy are discussed, as well as Hans

Delbrück's argument that there is no single employment doctrine for warfare.

Naval Doctrine Command in Norfolk, VA has 42 distribution list members for pure "maneuver" warfare.

Naval Doctrine Command has divisions in Norfolk, VA and Quantico, VA, with Australian, British, Canadian, French, and Italian Liaison Officers. It also has the Library-Naval Historical Center in Washington Navy Yard.

Joint Warfighting Center, Joint Electronic Library, Joint Doctrine Division, Air Force Doctrine Center, Headquarters Joint Doctrine Division, Library-Center for Naval Analyses, Armed Forces Staff College, Department of Operations Research, Naval Postgraduate School, Industrial College of the Armed Forces, National Strategy Decision-Making Department, Naval War College.

Commander Joe Kidd, RN, Director Naval Staff Duties Room 68 86, Ministry of Defence, Whitehall London SW1A 2MB sends air mail to Professor Eugenia Kiesling, Department of History, University of Alabama Box 870212, Tuscaloosa AL 35487-0212; Commander Alfredo Maglietta, ITN Administrative Assistant to the Commander Italian Naval War College Livorno, Italy; Dr. Edward J. Marolda, Head Contemporary History Branch Naval Historical Center Building 57 Washington Navy Yard 900 M Street SE Washington DC 200300; CAPT Jack McCaffrie, RAN Director General Maritime Studies Program ANZAC Park West APW2-G-11 Department of Defence Canberra ACT 2600 Australia; and CAPT Ryan McCombie USN ATTN: USAWC/AWC-J Army War College Carlisle Barracks, PA 17013-5050 and LT Dave Mirra USMC Doctrine Division - C42 Marine Corps send air mail.

MCMDC, Quantico, VA; AWC/DFX, Maxwell AFB, AL; TACTRAGRU, Dam Neck, VA; NDU-INSS-ROSA, Ft. McNair, DC; 1A, NWC-NWFA, Ft. McNair, DC; UK via air mail.

Col. Jon StUli, Lt.Cdr. John Taxeras, Dr. Geoffrey Till, Dr. Milan Vego, Cdr. Michael Vitale, Capt. George Wilson at Pentagon Room 4E367; CNA 440 Ford Ave, Alexandria VA; MCCDC 2076 South St,

Quantico VA; RNC Greenwich London SE1 0 9NN; NWC Newport RI 02841-5010; AWC 325 Chennault Circle, Maxwell AFB AL 36112-6427.

RECURSIVE SUMMARY ROUND 1

Naval doctrine involves pre-war doctrine, centralized doctrine, joint and multinational doctrine, NWP, French Navy doctrine, aircraft carriers, Sun Tz's influence, Delbrck's argument, and 42 distribution list members for maneuver warfare. It is subject to change and recommendations during war.

Liaison officers from Canada, France, and Italy, and various military organizations in the US, UK, Australia, and Italy are sending air mail to various recipients.

Pentagon Room 4E367; CNA, Alexandria VA; MCCDC, Quantico VA; RNC, London; NWC, Newport RI; AWC, Maxwell AFB AL.

RECURSIVE SUMMARY ROUND 2

Naval doctrine involves pre-war, centralized, joint, and multinational elements, with influence from Sun Tz and Delbrck. It is subject to change via air mail sent by liaison officers from various countries to recipients in the US, UK, Australia, and Italy.

Page-by-page Summaries

1. Navy doctrinal history and development discussed by Dr. James J. Tritten, approved for public release.

2. This report was prepared by the Naval Doctrine Command, and reviewed and released by staff. Reproduction is authorized.

3. Naval Doctrine Command report on lessons and conclusions from Navy and military doctrinal development; UNCLASSIFIED; 42 pages; 95,01,19; James J. Tritten, (804) 445-0565/6.

4. Study of military doctrine reveals lessons such as the importance of history, changing nature of doctrine, need for effectiveness measures, significance of joint and multinational doctrine, and the need for trained personnel and proper equipment.

5. Navy doctrine has been around since at least 1270, and was perfected by the time of the Battle of Lepanto in 1571. In the U.S., doctrine has been written and published for decades, and centralized doctrine was employed in World War II. Examples include pamphlets from Admirals Burke and Holloway.

6. US Navy doctrine existed in various forms and was demonstrated during the Battle of Leyte Gulf in 1944, when a small force of escorts courageously fought "against overwhelming odds."

7. Commodore Arleigh Burke, USN, used an informal doctrine and the initiative of his subordinates to turn back an enemy onslaught and ensure the survival of amphibious units and transports at Leyte Gulf. Other navies have developed formal written doctrine that the US Navy should consider when developing their own.

8. Studying the history of naval doctrine can provide doctrinal lessons, which are applicable despite technological advances. These include issues of attack, defense, and command and control, as well as integration of allies and coalition partners. There is a separate naval art and science, distinct from military art and science, which must be considered when writing navy doctrine.

9. The German Army in WWI had a sophisticated model for doctrinal development, which was inductive in its derivation and in application, and allowed for flexible application in the field. This allowed them to conserve resources and continue the war to 1918, while the German Navy lacked a concept of operations and had a rigid deductive doctrine which led to massive losses for the Allies in 1917.

10. German and French Army doctrines were incompatible and led to a French Army disaster. German doctrine emphasized decentralization and initiative, while French doctrine was centralized and emphasized control. There are doctrinal lessons to be learned from both the French and German Army, and the French Navy has a proud combat heritage. Doctrine can be learned from studying military history.

11	Research military history to understand the importance of doctrine and the need for a commander to follow it, and the reasons behind Admiral Byng's court-martial.
12	The Navy has had to operate within an established doctrine for centuries, but changes in technology and the end of the Anglo-Franco wars caused a shift in focus from doctrine to technology. Additionally, public debates among senior commanders following their victory in the Battle of Santiago may have discouraged open debate over doctrine.
13	Cervera was defeated in the Battle of Santiago due to a joint effort of land and sea forces, though it caused a public debate in the US Navy that lasted for years. Doctrine development is necessary for military success, but innovation in times of war is difficult.
14	The Royal Navy missed an opportunity to capitalize on the development of the light-weight radial aircraft engine for carrier warfare due to doctrinal rigidity. This rigidity caused a lack of appreciation for opportunities afforded by "revolutions in military affairs." Pre-war threat assessments and doctrine can often be wrong and must be adjusted for political and fiscal guidance.
15	Military doctrine should not be set in stone and must be subject to local commanders' interpretations. Deviations should be made with knowledge and judgement, and doctrine should be adapted in the face of combat losses.
16	Military doctrine must be flexible to accommodate changes in government and circumstances, and should be based on a consensus of experts with the right psychological traits. Doctrine should also transcend politics and be open to change.
17	Military doctrine should be developed from existing lessons of history, while also taking into account the opportunities presented by emerging technologies and new political realities.
18	The Imperial Japanese Navy gave more impetus to the development of night tactics and formed specialized night combat groupings to weaken the U.S. Pacific Fleet. Doctrinal changes in the U.S. and Royal Navy were the result of bureaucratic operations and it is important to be prepared for doctrinal change during a war.
19	Successful adaptation during combat is easier to accomplish when military doctrine is living and breathing. Case studies and books on innovation can provide guidance on how to achieve this.
20	Japan successfully changed their battle doctrine from battleships to aircraft carriers. The U.S. Marine Corps and French Navy also needed to make changes to their doctrines, and these changes were facilitated by the retirement of senior officers. New naval doctrines are largely based on the original 'From the Sea' document, and require both warriors and bureaucrats to be successful.
21	Organizations need to be created to monitor doctrine and foster new ideas, supported by a feedback system to measure

effectiveness. MOEs should consider success, acceptability, adaptability, consistency, relevancy, and attainability. Doctrine should be tailored to warfighting and programming.

22 Military doctrine must be based on observed capability of weapons systems and success of the program in a realistic combat environment. Doctrine may be culturally biased, and is often developed from the top down or by new technologies and battlefield successes. It can be written by many different people, and there is a tension between control and independence.

23 Navies have a lack of modern tradition of written doctrinal debate due to the relative degree of independence they are afforded. Civilians have been involved in nuclear and naval nuclear warfighting doctrine, while navies have been largely responsible for programs to field the weapons systems and operate them safely. The U.S. Army has a strong program of letting doctrinal ideas appear first as articles subject to debate and revision.

24 Joint doctrine and multinational doctrine are becoming increasingly important as militaries downsize and must work together to meet national objectives. U.S. Navy doctrine must be developed with the intention of sharing it with foreign navies.

25 Navy forces retain their sovereignty and are quickly able to revert to national control, whereas land forces are not subject to the same degree of residual control by their parent nations and require formal doctrine. There is a historical parallel between the knight on horseback and navy and aviation forces.

26 Nations with global responsibilities may have different military doctrines for different geographic areas and threats, and defense and attrition warfare may be more appropriate in some cases.

27 Sun Tzu and other ancient Chinese philosophers have influenced navy warfare, and their teachings on defense and offense have been explored by the Imperial Japanese Navy and other modern Western military nations. This understanding of potential enemies' culture is necessary to correctly predict and interpret their military and naval doctrine. The first division of warfare into annihilation and attrition was by Raimondo Montecuccoli in the 17th Century.

28 Helmuth von Moltke and Alfred von Schlieffen developed the concept of a decisive battle of annihilation and Hans Delbrück further refined the concept of annihilation and attrition. Aleksandr A. Svechin wrote a treatise on the two types of warfare and this concept was used in War Plan Orange. It has been used by various commanders in history, and some were criticized for not exploiting the victory.

29 Admiral William Halsey's decision to seek out the enemy's carriers at the Battle of Leyte Gulf was influenced by his victory at the Battle of the Philippine Sea. Doctrine must include ruthless strategies to achieve the desired end state of annihilating an enemy surface fleet. Maneuver warfare is a philosophy of warfare that supports both annihilation and attrition warfare.

30 The French Navy's doctrinal literature provides lessons for navies to develop formal written doctrine for warfighting, independent naval campaigns, and joint/multinational operations. The U.S. Navy and Marine Corps have published their initial multi-Service doctrinal publication, Naval Warfare.

31 Naval Warfare establishes principles of offensive and maneuver warfare, emphasizes the importance of joint and multinational operations, and requires the development of doctrine beyond technology. Doctrine needs to be supported with resources and adequately explained to governments for the military to be successful.

32 Political leaders must be careful not to bias military doctrine writers towards the offensive, and military professionals must factor all other inputs and inform political leadership of risks involved with the offensive. Simulations, games, and exercises can help to validate doctrinal theories, and good doctrine and training can lead to success in battle. Naval doctrine can present a target for change, but is necessary for self-regulating operations.

33 Military doctrine is a combination of current policy, available resources, strategy, threats, history, technology, geography, and government type, and affects how we fight, train, exercise, organize, buy, and plan. It must be evaluated and questioned to ensure it is the correct doctrine for the future.

34 Naval doctrine is a multi-service perspective of how the naval services think about and act during war and military operations. It is evolving and dynamic while capturing enduring elements, and should be associated with leadership training and education.

35 Naval doctrine is a fundamental principle of naval thought and practice that guides admirals and commanders in warfare. It is composed of experiences from similar situations and affects all ranks. Without doctrinal direction, naval warfare would not succeed.

36 The Atlantic Convoy Instructions (1941 or 1942) codified multi-carrier task force operations and updated USF-10 due to combat experience, and have been accepted as doctrine by the US Navy. Spruance and Halsey's decisions at the Battle of the Philippine Sea and Battle of Leyte Gulf have been compared to USF-10 and PAC-10, which dictate the commander's actions.

37 A discussion of naval power in the Middle East, with reference to European and Naval Arms Control in the Gorbachev Era, the Basic Aerospace Doctrine of the US Air Force, On War by Clausewitz, and various other works.

38 British, Russian, and Chinese military doctrine is placed between military policy and military art/strategy, having both political and military-technical aspects. Western military doctrine is studied but not for navy doctrine. Admiral Knox's "Role of Doctrine in Naval Warfare" (1915) and Major General Holley's lecture (1994) discussed doctrine. Admiral Boorda (1994) discussed people and technology. Historical examples of doctrine include Admiral

Nelson's captains (1798-1805), Admiral Sampson and Santiago (1898), and Admiral Schley and Santiago (1898).

39 Colonel Jablonsky, Admiral Lanxada, Aspin, Captain Moore, Dr. Hata, General Franks, Rear Admiral Lewis, McCaulley and Major General Willcocks discuss military and religious doctrine.

40 Evans & Peattie (1994) and Delbrück (1920, 1923, 1985) discuss Imperial Japanese Navy strategy, tactics and technology, as well as medieval and modern warfare. Melhorn (1974) and Allard (1994) discuss aircraft carrier development and U.S. naval doctrine respectively. Reckner (forthcoming) will provide further research on U.S. naval doctrine. Lupfer (1987) discusses German tactical doctrine in WWI.

41 Paul S. Dull, Geoffrey Till, Stephen Peter Rosen, Harold R. Winton, John D. Harbron, David C. Evans & Mark R. Peattie, Department of the Navy, Norman Friedman, Thomas C. Hone & Mark D. Mandeles, Irving J. Brinton Holley, Jr., Jeremy M. Boorda, and Maxwell Thurman discuss the history and implementation of naval strategy, tactics and technology.

42 Major General I. B. Holley Jr. suggests steps for doctrinal process, J. J. Tritten discusses whether naval warfare is unique, H. Delbrück examines the art of war in Volumes II and III, H. R. Winton studies difficulty in changing British Army doctrine, J. M. Collins examines military preparedness, A. Savelyev discusses Russia's need for a potential enemy, G. Y. Akavia and D. C. Evans and M. R. Peattie research defensive defense and naval strategy, and N. Dixon and S. Tzu provide thought-provoking discourses on military topics.

43 FMFM 1 (1989), Seven Military Classics of Ancient China (1993), Tao Te Ching (1988), influence of Sun Tzu on Japanese Imperial Navy (1990), Posen's offensive/defensive military doctrine (1984), Maurice of Nassau, Gustavus Adolphus, Montecuccoli & military revolution (1986), Moltke, Schlieffen & doctrine of strategic envelopment (1986), Delbruck (1986), Geyer on German strategy (1986), Rice on Soviet strategy (1986), Svechin on strategy (1992), and Ohmae on Battle of Savo Island (n.d.).

44 Various authors discuss the use of maneuver warfare, maritime strategy, and military doctrine in World War II.

45 Akavia (1993) examines cults in French military thought before 1914. Toffler (1993) suggests stretching one's mind. Arellano & Kohout (1993) discuss the revolutionary/evolutionary role of Naval Doctrine Command.

46 Naval Doctrine Command, 1540 Gilbert St., Norfolk, VA, has Commander (00), Deputy Commander (01), Science Advisor (02SA), Technical and Financial Division (02T), Center for Naval Analyses Rep. (02EG), Naval Doctrine Dev. Div. (N3), Joint/Combined Doctrine Div. (N5), Evaluation, Training, and Education Div. (N7), Strategy and Concepts Div. (N8), Health Service Support Div. (N9, 2200 Lester St., Quantico, VA).

47 Dr. James J. Tritten (N5A) and various international liaison officers at Naval Doctrine Command, 1540 Gilbert Street, Norfolk, VA 23511-2785. Joint Warfighting Center, Joint Electronic Library (JEL), Air Force Doctrine Center, and Joint Doctrine Division for U.S. Army Training and Doctrine Command at various locations.

48 Library locations for Naval Analyses, Armed Forces Staff College, Defense Technical Information Center, CEMA, Naval War College, Office of the Command Historian, Congressional Research Service, Naval Postgraduate School, and Commission Francaise d'Histoire Maritime.

49 CAPT Alain Delbury, FN (SACLANT); CAPT Hughes de Longevialle, FN (Embassy of France); RADM J.L. Duval, FN (Centre d'Enseignement Superieur de la Marine); CAPT Theodore Ferriter, USN (ALSA Center); CAPT Thom Ford, USN (US Army Command); RADM Jose Ignacio Gonzalez-Aller Hierro, SPN (Museo Naval de Madrid); CAPT Jaime Goyeness, SPN (Spanish Military Mission to SACLANT); Dr. Thomas Grassey (Naval War College Review); Eric J. Grove (Centre for Security Studies); Dr. John Hattendorf (Advanced Research Department).

50 LTG I.B. Holley (Duke), CAPT Wayne Hughes (NPS), Dr. John H. Johns (Industrial College), Professor Kevin Kelly (NWC), Commander Joe Kidd (UK), Professor Eugenia Kiesling (Alabama), Commander Alfredo Maglietta (Italy), Dr. Edward J. Marolda (Naval Historical Center).

51 Andrew Marshall (OSD/NA, Pentagon Room 3A930) directs Net Assessment for Office of the Secretary of Defense; Professeur Philippe Masson (Service Historique de la Marine, Chateau de Vincennes, France) and CAPT Jack McCaffrie (Director General, Maritime Studies Program, Department of Defence, Australia) contacted; CAPT Ryan McCombie (USAWC/AWC-J, Army War College, PA), LTC Dave Mirra (Doctrine Division - C42, MCCDC, VA), Dr. James A. Mowbray (Code AWC/DFX, Air War College, AL), CAPT Christopher Nelson (Ret., TACTRAGRULANT, VA), CAPT Michael F. O'Brien (Code: NDU-INSS-ROSA, Institute for National Strategic Studies, NDU, DC) contacted.

52 CAPT Chris Page, RN (Head of Defence Studies, Ministry of Defence, London, UK); CAPT John N. Petrie, USN (Director of Writing & Research, National War College, Washington, DC); Dr. Bruce Powers (Office of the Chief of Naval Operations, Pentagon); COL Jon StUli, USMC (Armed Forces Staff College, Norfolk, VA); CAPT Peter Swartz, USN (Ret.) (Center for Naval Analyses, Alexandria, VA); LTC John Taxeras, USMC (Marine Corps University, Quantico, VA); Dr. Geoffrey Till (Department of History and International Affairs, Royal Naval College Greenwich, London, UK); Dr. Milan Vego (Department of Operations, Naval War College, Newport, RI).

53 CDR Michael Vitale, USN at The Pentagon, and CAPT George Wilson, USN at Air War College, Maxwell AFB.

Moods

Figure 1. [Black and white pen and ink sketch. Illustrate the mood felt as a result of failures in naval doctrine.] Nimble Books AI using Stable Diffusion. If I am interpreting this correctly, the AI has rendered the ship unarmed, with its radars facing backwards.

Figure 2. DALL-E, same prompt. A hazy, distorted view of an obsolete, decrepit warship at port.

3-00-007

NAVAL DOCTRINE COMMAND
Norfolk, Virginia

Lessons and Conclusions From the History of Navy and Military Doctrinal Development

by

Dr. James J. Tritten

January 1995

DTIC QUALITY INSPECTED 3

Approved for public release; distribution unlimited.

19950206 213

NAVAL DOCTRINE COMMAND
Norfolk Virginia

Rear Admiral F.L. Lewis
Commander

The work reported herein was prepared by the Naval Doctrine Command. This report reflects the opinion of the author only and does not represent the views or policies of the Naval Doctrine Command, the U.S. Navy and Marine Corps, or the Department of Defense.

Reproduction of all or part of this report is authorized.

This report was prepared by:

DR. JAMES JOHN TRITTEN
Joint/Combined Doctrine Division

Reviewed by;

JOHN D. WOODS, COL, USMC
Division Director
Joint/Combined Doctrine Division

Released by;

C. M. deGRUY, CAPT, USN
Chief of Staff

REPORT DOCUMENTATION PAGE

Form Approved
OMB No. 0704-0188

1a. REPORT SECURITY CLASSIFICATION UNCLASSIFIED	**1b. RESTRICTIVE MARKINGS**
2a. SECURITY CLASSIFICATION AUTHORITY	**3. DISTRIBUTION/AVAILABILITY OF REPORT** APPROVED FOR PUBLIC RELEASE; DISTRIBUTION UNLIMITED
2b. CLASSIFICATION/DOWNGRADING SCHEDULE	
4. PERFORMING ORGANIZATION REPORT NUMBER(S) NDC 3-00-007	**5. MONITORING ORGANIZATION REPORT NUMBER(S)**
6a. NAME OF PERFORMING ORGANIZATION NAVAL DOCTRINE COMMAND	**6b. OFFICE SYMBOL** N5A	**7a. NAME OF MONITORING ORGANIZATION**
6c. ADDRESS (CITY, STATE, AND ZIP CODE) 1540 GILBERT STREET NORFOLK, VA 23511-2785	**7b. ADDRESS (CITY, STATE, AND ZIP CODE)**
8a. NAME OF FUNDING/SPONSORING ORGANIZATION	**8b. OFFICE SYMBOL**	**9. PROCUREMENT INSTRUMENT IDENTIFICATION NUMBER**
8c. ADDRESS (CITY, STATE, AND ZIP CODE)	**10. SOURCE OF FUNDING NUMBERS** PROGRAM ELEMENT NO. / PROJECT NO. / TASK NO. / WORK UNIT ACCESSION NO.

11. TITLE (INCLUDE SECURITY CLASSIFICATION)
LESSONS AND CONCLUSIONS FROM THE HISTORY OF NAVY AND MILITARY DOCTRINAL DEVELOPMENT

12. PERSONAL AUTHOR(S)
DR. JAMES J. TRITTEN

13a. TYPE OF REPORT	13b. TIME COVERED	14. DATE OF REPORT (YY,MM,DD)	15. PAGE COUNT
FINAL	FROM FEB 94 TO JAN 95	95,01,19	42

16. SUPPLEMENTARY NOTATION

17. COSATI CODES			18. SUBJECT TERMS (Continue on reverse if necessary and identify by block number)
FIELD	GROUP	SUB-GROUP	DOCTRINE, MILITARY DOCTRINE, TACTICS, NAVAL DOCTRINE, STRATEGY, TECHNOLOGY, NAVY DOCTRINE, OPERATIONAL ART

19. ABSTRACT (CONTINUE ON REVERSE IF NECESSARY AND IDENTIFY BY BLOCK NUMBER)

THERE ARE SOME EXCELLENT LESSONS TO BE LEARNED CONCERNING THE DEVELOPMENT OF MILITARY DOCTRINE BY NAVIES IN THE WORLD. THESE LESSONS INCLUDE: THAT NAVY DOCTRINE HAS EXISTED IN THE PAST [IT IS NOT NEW]; IT IS PROPER TO STUDY THE DOCTRINAL LESSONS OF OTHER NATIONS AND OTHER SERVICES; IMPORTANT DOCTRINAL LESSONS CAN BE DRAWN FROM HISTORY; FORMAL NAVY DOCTRINE SUFFERED A SETBACK WITH THE INTRODUCTION OF NEW TECHNOLOGIES AND THE END OF THE ANGLO-FRANCO WARS; PRE-WAR MILITARY DOCTRINE CANNOT FORSEE ALL EVENTUALITIES; CENTRALIZED MILITARY DOCTRINE SHOULD NOT BE CAST IN STONE; MILITARY DOCTRINE HAS CHANGED DUE TO A VARIETY OF CIRCUMSTANCES; IT IS NOT EASY TO INSTITUTE A SIGNIFICANT DOCTRINAL CHANGE IN LARGE ORGANIZATIONS; IT APPEARS EASIER TO CHANGE MILITARY DOCTRINE WHEN IT IS WRITTEN; MEASURES OF EFFECTIVENESS ARE NEEDED FOR MILITARY DOCTRINE; SUCCESSFUL NAVY DOCTRINE HAS BEEN PREPARED BY A VARIETY OF INDIVIDUALS; DOCTRINE MUST BE MEANINGFUL; JOINT AND MULTINATIONAL DOCTRINE BECOME MORE IMPORTANT AS NATIONAL FORCES DOWNSIZE; MULTINATIONAL DOCTRINE FOR NAVY FORCES WILL BE INHERENTLY DIFFERENT THAN MULTINATIONAL DOCTRINE FOR LAND FORCES; THERE IS NO ONE CORRECT MILITARY DOCTRINE; THERE IS A DOCTRINAL RENAISSANCE IN PROGRESS; GOOD MILITARY DOCTRINE IS OF NO VALUE WITHOUT GOOD MEN AND WOMEN WHO ARE TRAINED AND PROVIDED THE PROPER EQUIPMENT; AND NAVAL DOCTRINE IS NOT RISK FREE.

20. DISTRIBUTION/AVAILABILITY OF ABSTRACT X UNCLASSIFIED/UNLIMITED __ SAME AS RPT. __ DTIC USERS	21. ABSTRACT SECURITY CLASSIFICATION UNCLASSIFIED	
22a. NAME OF RESPONSIBLE INDIVIDUAL JAMES J. TRITTEN	22b. TELEPHONE (INCLUDE AREA CODE) (804) 445-0565/6	22c. OFFICE SYMBOL N5A

DD FORM 1473, 84 MAR

Previous editions are obsolete.

SECURITY CLASSIFICATION OF THIS PAGE

S/N 0102-LF-014-6603

LESSONS AND CONCLUSIONS FROM THE HISTORY OF NAVY AND MILITARY DOCTRINAL DEVELOPMENT

by

James J. Tritten[1]

There are some excellent lessons to be learned concerning the development of military doctrine by navies in the world. These lessons include: that navy doctrine has existed in the past [it is not new]; it is proper to study the doctrinal lessons of other nations and other services; important doctrinal lessons can be drawn from history; formal navy doctrine suffered a setback with the introduction of new technologies and the end of the Anglo-Franco wars; pre-war military doctrine cannot foresee all eventualities; centralized military doctrine should not be cast in stone; military doctrine has changed due to a variety of circumstances; it is not easy to institute a significant doctrinal change in large organizations; it appears easier to change military doctrine when it is written; measures of effectiveness are needed for military doctrine; successful navy doctrine has been prepared by a variety of individuals; doctrine must be meaningful; joint doctrine and multinational doctrine become more important as national forces downsize; multinational doctrine for navy forces will be inherently different than multinational doctrine for land forces; there is no one correct military doctrine; there is a doctrinal renaissance in progress; good military doctrine is of no value without good men and women who are trained and provided the proper equipment; and naval doctrine is not risk free.

This list of lessons is drawn from a consideration of what constitutes naval and military doctrine[1] and the initial part of a comprehensive review of the historical case studies of doctrine in other navies and other Services.[2] Evidence of military and navy doctrine can be found in primary source material--actual written materials of a doctrinal nature, a review of past combat and after-action assessments, and by considering actual force postures. As additional cases are developed and existing cases are refined, these lessons will be re-evaluated and scrutinized to see if they stand the test of new and additional information. In the meantime, they should be taken to heart by military doctrine commands and by new doctrine writers.

---

[1] The views expressed by the author are his alone and do not necessarily represent those of the U.S. government, Department of Defense, or the U.S. Navy. The author would like to acknowledge the contributions of Captain Wayne Hughes, USN (Ret.), at the Naval Postgraduate School; Captain Peter Swartz, USN (Ret.), at the Center for Naval Analyses; Dr. Susan Canedy, U.S. Army Training and Doctrine Command (TRADOC); Captain Robert Bathurst, USN (Ret.), at the International Peace Research Institute (PRIO), in Oslo, Norway; and Dr. Charles Meconis, at the Institute for Global Security Studies, Seattle, WA.

The History of Navy Doctrine

Navy doctrine has existed in the past--in Spain at least since 1270.[3] Fighting instructions were known to have been issued by various naval commanders operating in Renaissance Venice during the age of galleys. One of the earliest of these efforts are the *Orders and Signals* of the Venetian Fleet in 1365.[4] These orders included specific operational formations as well as signals indicating the fleet commander's intent. Italian city-states fielded fleets led by admirals, such as Genoa's Andrea Doria, with a world-wide reputation. By the time of the Battle of Lepanto (1571), the doctrine and tactics of galley warfare in the Mediterranean had been perfected to such a state that each side could be considered masters of the naval art.

Navy and multi-Service naval doctrine has existed, under other names, in all navies of the world. All professions have doctrine and the military is a profession which, like all other professions, has to have had doctrine. In addition to formal written navy doctrine, of which there is ample abundance, informal and unwritten customary navy doctrine has existed as a shared culture of fundamental principles of thought and actions in the minds of its admirals and commanders. By reviewing the actions of the military profession, as well as the after-action reports and courts-martial, we are able to ascertain the doctrine of that profession even if it was not formally written. Both formal and informal doctrine can serve to define what a profession thinks and how it acts. When unwritten, professions operating without written doctrine more resemble a jazz group jamming rather than an orchestra following written sheet music and led by a conductor.[5] Both practices result in music.

What is new today for the U.S. Navy is the institution of a formal centralized doctrine command and doctrinal process on the model of the Army's Training and Doctrine Command (TRADOC). It is *not* the first time that the U.S. naval Services have attempted formal multi-Service naval doctrine nor the first time that doctrine for the naval Services has been formalized or written.[6] Doctrine for the U.S. Navy has been written and published for many decades over our long history.

Current conventional wisdom says that the U.S. Navy never has had a centralized military doctrine. In point of fact, the U.S. Pacific Fleet in World War II operated under centralized war instructions, centralized general tactical instructions, *U.S. Fleet Doctrine and Tactical Orders (USF-10)*, *Current Tactical Orders and Doctrine U.S. Pacific Fleet (PAC-10)*, and type doctrines and tactical orders prepared for each class of ship.[7] Written and centralized multinational navy doctrine existed in the Atlantic theater during World War II.[8] The British and French Navies adopted many forms of U.S. Navy doctrine during the war. This written doctrine documented how commanders operated their forces at sea to win against a determined enemy engaged in mortal combat. Having written Navy doctrine did *not* detract from our victory at sea or the many victories of other navies.

Two more recent examples are a pamphlet issued by Admiral Arleigh Burke, USN, Chief of Naval Operations, *Origins of United States Navy Doctrine*, and a similar one by Admiral James L. Holloway III, USN, *Planning, Readiness and Employment Doctrine for*

U.S. Naval Operating Forces.[9] Even when the Naval Doctrine Command (NDC) was stood up, formal centralized written Navy doctrine existed in the form of Naval Warfare Publication [NWP]-1, *Strategic Concepts of the U.S. Navy*.

Navy doctrine existed also in many other forms when NDC began its operations. Written Navy doctrine already existed as the Navy component of joint and multinational doctrine as well as existing Marine Corps Service-specific doctrine. Formal written functional doctrine existed in the construct of doctrine for amphibious warfare and various specific combat arms in the form of various tactical notes and memos. Although NDC is the first multi-Service naval doctrine command, it is not the first military command which has written American naval doctrine; the doctrine division at the Marine Corps Combat Development Command (MCCDC) and joint doctrine preceded the establishment of NDC by some years. Before that, doctrine was prepared at major naval commands and in Washington, DC.

Basic principles of beliefs and practices do not have to be written to be doctrine. Unwritten customary informal Navy doctrine has existed and still exists in the form of commander's intent, and the shared experiences of the existing officer corps, especially its admirals and commanders. When faced with situations that were not foreseen in the pre-battle Operations Orders, Navy officers have intuitively known what needed to be done and then acted in accordance with that unwritten doctrine to fight as bravely as necessary to ensure victory.

For example, during the engagement off Samar Island at the Battle of Leyte Gulf (1944), most U.S. Navy ships and aircraft were out of communication with each other for extended periods of time and the situation encountered was not foreseen in any Operations Order or pre-war battle simulation or exercise and without centralized written doctrine. Yet the small force destined to defend the landing force at Leyte Gulf managed to successfully operate together in some of the heaviest fighting ever seen at sea.

Admiral Clifton A.F. Sprague's small escort carriers, their embarked air groups, and the sailors on destroyers and destroyer escorts fought "against overwhelming odds from which survival could not be expected."[10] When the destroyer *Johnston* saw a squadron of four enemy destroyers and a light cruiser coming in to attack the carriers and complete the boxing-in of the American defending force, her captain seized the offensive and took on the whole squadron despite being out of torpedoes.[11] Her furious close-in gunfire attacks so startled the enemy that the enemy's torpedoes were launched prematurely and caused no damage. Aircraft pilots from the escort carriers continued to make attack runs against enemy surface forces when their ammunition was exhausted in order to force a reaction. Other aircraft flew to shore airfields or any deck that could take them in order to rearm and rejoin the fray.

All of this was done because the officers in command knew that their role was to protect the bigger ships and all the ships were to protect the landing force--even at the cost of their own lives. At the end of the engagement, a small but brave force of escorts had courageously turned back the onslaught of enemy battleships, heavy and light cruisers, and destroyers and ensured the survival of the amphibious units and transports at Leyte Gulf. Without having a dedicated plan to execute and being without tactical communications to order about forces, it was the individual commander's intuitive knowledge of how to fight and his assessment of what needed to be done that carried the day.

Commodore Arleigh Burke, USN much like Admiral Lord Horatio Nelson before him, chose to rely on a personal doctrine and the initiative of his subordinates. During World War II, Burke held a series of meetings with his commanders in which ideas and information were exchanged and doctrine was established. When the battle occurred, very few orders needed to be issued since each commander thoroughly understood what was expected in various circumstances.[12] There is a long history of the informal beliefs of the officer corps as doctrine. Such informal doctrine may even be more powerful than the official written versions which coexist. The parallel in international law is law based upon custom and not on treaties. Both are equally valid but treaties are easier to change.

It is acceptable to **study the doctrinal lessons of other navies and other Services** and then to borrow from them--just as we routinely borrow each other's technology. In part, this is what the U.S. Navy did when it learned about aircraft carriers from the Royal Navy and what the Royal Navy did when it integrated their carrier force within the U.S. Pacific Fleet in World War II.[13] One respected student of the Royal Navy, Captain S.W. Roskill, RN (Ret.) openly credits French sources as having a "very marked[ly]" influence on tactical thought in the Royal Navy.[14] The Soviet Navy studied the Royal Navy's performance in the Falklands War, in part, to learn from the experience and especially to see how one might use their new limited-capability aircraft carriers to support an operational-level military action in distant waters. Japanese Navy doctrine freely borrowed from mainland China, Great Britain, and from its own ancient pirate heritage.[15] The U.S. Navy never developed functional doctrine for chemical warfare defense ashore due to the existing expertise within the U.S. Army and their supporting doctrinal literature. In the 1980s, the U.S. Army War College used a paper written by a U.S. Navy officer in 1915 as assigned readings on the concept of military doctrine.[16]

The concept of formal written doctrine for the U.S. Navy is one that we are borrowing from the Spanish, the Italians, the British and the French. There are other navies in the world today that have previously thought through navy doctrine, under various titles, that we should consider when we develop our new American doctrine. For example, we should study the use of navy power by Arabs and the Israelis as we shift to littoral warfare.[17] Why not look at foreign experiences with full recognition that not all lessons learned will be valid to our own circumstances?

We should fully expect that nations with less developed navies will study the lessons of history and borrow those tried and proven elements of doctrine that appear to work well against larger navies. For example, there is an extremely well-developed theory of *manoeuvre* warfare doctrine that was developed by the French after long years of warfare against the superior Royal Navy. Smaller navies could easily use this doctrine as the model upon which to base their own tactical-level engagements against the superior U.S. Navy.

The Value of Studying the History of Navy Doctrine

Important doctrinal lessons can be drawn from history, even from the age of sail. For example, from even a cursory study of the past, it is apparent that major current doctrinal issues have been debated during eras of greatly different technology. These include: (1), what is the principal form of attack; (2), what is the object of the attack--the escorted ships or its escorts; (3), how much of the attacking force should be withheld in reserve; (4), is the war essentially one of annihilation or attrition; (5), what is more important in defense--the protection of escorted ships (or an invasion force) or the defeat of an enemy's offensive fighting power; (6), how should navies fight in the littoral (most naval warfare has been here); (7), what should the command and control relationships be as naval forces project power ashore; (8), how to integrate allies and ad hoc coalition partners to achieve a single purpose; (9) how far should the combat commander on the scene comply with doctrine issued by bureaucracies ashore; and (10), how much should the commander rely upon enemy intentions versus capabilities? These are not new issues, but rather doctrinal issues of how to fight that cross national, geographic, and technology boundaries and have been debated for hundreds of years.[18] To attempt to write navy doctrine without a serious review of this history would be imprudent, at best. When trying to write substantive navy doctrine, these are the tough issues that one must deal with if the product is to be taken seriously.

There is a tendency in the United States to view military art and military science as all-encompassing terms that include warfare in all possible dimensions.[19] At the apex of theoretical studies of military art and military science are books such as Clausewitz's *On War*.[20] Within such books are doctrinal principles which have been accepted by ground forces but may be totally inappropriate for navy and other forces.[21] For example, Clausewitz teaches us that the defensive is the stronger form of warfare--despite historical examples to the contrary, such as Julius Caesar's conquests.[22] A review of navy warfare history also suggests otherwise. A review of air warfare and the theory of nuclear warfare likewise suggests that the offensive form of war is stronger than the defense. Yet we are trapped in a paradigm of military art that teaches us that the defense is stronger. Perhaps the real issue is that there is a separate and equally important naval art and naval science that parallels military art and military science.

A serious review of navy doctrinal development cannot help but demonstrate the major differences between lessons learned from studying ground and maritime examples. In studying historical examples, it is easy to get sidetracked into culturally-biased preconceptions about other Services and nations based upon historical track records of combat prowess. In looking for lessons learned, we need not allow such prejudice influence our thinking. After all, it is not our objective to study combat success but rather bureaucratic behavior and sound thinking. For example, the Soviet Union had a long-standing history of good military theory and planning but an equally long record of poor execution at the tactical and operational-levels of warfare coupled with strategic success. We have studied and adopted much from the Russian ground forces model without letting that study impact our thoughts on warfare at sea.

Similarly, Germany has a long record of sound thinking and good execution at the tactical and operational-levels of warfare with defeat at the strategic level--and we continue to study them today. Despite the desire of ground forces to continue to study the lessons of German ground forces, we wisely ignore the poor examples from the lessons on German Navy doctrinal development. Indeed, the abolition of the German Admiralty in 1889 by Kaiser Wilhelm II and the subsequent justification by Alfred von Tirpitz of naval strategy and doctrine by reference to Karl von Clausewitz is a model of how not to develop sound navy doctrine as proven by World War I. Despite sound planing for ground warfare in France, the German military did not even have a concept of operations for the fleet to contest control of the seas, or for that matter anything, in support of the Schlieffen plan.

The general model for doctrinal development in the German Army during World War I was quite sophisticated.[23] When the war did not develop according to pre-war predictions, *die Oberste Heeresleitung* (the Army High Command) solicited and approved a new doctrine of defense in depth which allowed them to conserve resources and continue the war to 1918 when they were able to mass forces for a major offensive. The process of making these changes was extremely dynamic and incorporated from independent experimentation in the field. When the new doctrine was approved, it was accompanied by new equipment, reorganization, and training.

With the new opportunities afforded by their conservation of resources, the Germans once again sought inputs for a new offensive doctrine of the breakthrough and successfully published one in time for the 1918 offensive. This offensive doctrine made full use of the lessons learned in the field from both the allied and German perspective. This "maneuver" warfare offensive doctrine was quite successful on the battlefield but failed in the face of overwhelming numbers of allied forces.

The Germans in World War I treated change with respect, but, once change was accepted, it was pursued with ardor. No change in doctrine was considered workable unless the Army could see how it was to be implemented. This implied a strong correlation between doctrine and training. Despite the thoroughness in the adoption of doctrine, the applications of doctrine in the field under unique battlefield conditions was flexible enough to allow individual judgment by the commander. The Germans made the distinction between techniques, which are taught and rigid, and tactics, which allow for creativity. Doctrine for the German Army was inductive in its derivation and in application. Doctrine for the allied armies was deductive, more rigid, and became the formula for the massive losses of personnel during their 1917 offensive.

We apparently have much to learn from German Army doctrinal history and much less from German Navy history. For example, German Army doctrine during the inter-War years, was based upon two field service regulations issued in 1921 and 1933.[24] German doctrine emphasized maneuver, mobility, the offensive, surprise, tempo, and the penetration of enemy defenses. Indeed, Army doctrine was for one continuous battle with the commitment of reserves to ensure that the enemy was overwhelmed and momentum was not lost. French Army doctrine, on the other hand, saw the battle on the field as a series of successive methodical battles. These doctrines were incompatible and the obsolete doctrine of the French Army drove a flawed strategy that resulted in a catastrophe.

German Army doctrine also emphasized decentralization and initiative at the lowest levels of the chain of command. German Army doctrine emphasized the *auftragstakik*, or mission-oriented tactics that permitted the lower-echelon commander to operate within his seniors intent. An officer could ignore standing directives, naturally at his own risk, if he were responding to local conditions. French Army doctrine was centralized and emphasized control. As a result of their doctrine, the German could count on locally-initiated counterattacks while fighting on the defensive. The French Army needed to be ordered into a counterattack.

Yet despite this apparent value in studying the German example, there is not much to learn there from a perspective of Navy doctrine. Yet there is a great deal to be learned from French Navy doctrine. The myth of French military performance on the battlefield or of French Army doctrine in no ways denigrates the proud combat heritage of the Navy of the *ancien régime* and the excellent doctrinal development that has long-characterized the French Navy. Unfortunately, most of that story has never been adequately translated into English and been internalized by the U.S. Navy officer corps, who views its cultural antecedent as the Royal Navy. Quite frankly, the performance and heritage of the French Army has been allowed to cloud the opinion of U.S. Navy officers about the French Navy in an altogether unwarranted fashion. In the words of a well-respected scholar, "...France has had little just cause to be ashamed of her navy: the navy may have had some just cause to be ashamed of France."[25]

We have a rich sound naval and military history from which to draw important doctrinal lessons of interest today. This will not be easy, since most military history books do not index the term doctrine and many others use the term to refer to higher level political policy guidance.[26] Simply put, there will be a great deal of hard work during which scholars will need to review military history (how navies have acted) and extract from it the doctrinal lessons. Having done this, it will be much easier to develop new navy doctrine, since we will obviously find that many of the issues under consideration today, have been researched and thoroughly debated before.

Military doctrine can be learned and serves to assist the commander, even if it has not been formally written. The early Italian campaign of Napoleon Bonaparte was conducted without formal written doctrine. Yet those officers who participated in the campaign were "indoctrinated" with new concepts and methods of warfare, giving them an advantage over those who had served elsewhere.[27] The key to finding such doctrine is to study the actions of the military force and then verify from the after action reports that the commander was not court-martialed for his actions.

When searching through the lessons learned, doctrinal writers need to be aware of the full data base available on any particular doctrinal issue. Where there is a reasonably large sample, they should avoid the extremes and instead concentrate on the bell curve majority.[28] There will obviously be problems with rejecting the extremes, just as there were problems in the 1980s with assessments regarding Soviet military capability. Just as then, the formation of "B" teams of outsiders might also be instructive.

Equally importantly, there have been unintended doctrinal developments due to incomplete understanding of history. First, for example, many navy officers in many countries have thought that Nelson succeeded because he <u>ignored</u> the fighting instructions of the day. This has resulted in a feeling that one simply needs to get into combat and "mix it up" in a *mêlée* like Nelson did, or his French counterpart Vice Admiral Pierre André, Bailli de Suffren-Saint Tropez, or the earlier Spanish Captain-General Don Álvaro de Bazán, Marqués de Santa Cruz. Such thinking appears to have come about recently with a shift to aircraft as the principal striking arm of the fleet.

A more accurate accounting of history is that Nelson <u>followed</u> the fighting instructions, more often than not and, moreover, he expected his captains to follow <u>his</u> directions. Nelson's "touch" lay in his different style of Navy doctrine that was appropriate for the time, place, and the "band of brothers" with which he served.[29] No military can operate with all, or even most, of its officers operating outside of the doctrine of the profession. A single commander can more easily operate outside of the norms--and continue to do so as long as he succeeds at the missions and tasks that he has been assigned. In general, a military has to have a doctrine for its routine operations that are the basis from which one may depart. If the commander chooses to deviate from established standards, he will then know that he has done so and know what that means.[30]

A second incomplete lesson from history has to do with the death of Admiral Sir John Byng. Byng was <u>not</u> shot for failing to mindlessly follow doctrine. This myth seems to have permeated a number of officer corps and helped perpetuate the idea that formal, centralized, written doctrine is <u>not</u> in their best interests. Admiral Byng was shot, and the adherence to fighting instructions was an issue in his court martial--but the issue is far more complicated. Byng was shot because the British government needed a scapegoat for his actions and the loss of Minorca in 1756.

There are many extremely important lessons learned from our past experiences that we can draw upon today. As we re-integrate the submarine forces back into the fleet as integral units of task groups, there is a rich history of previous experience of that type upon which we should draw. Submarines were not always thought of as being "lone wolves" and the initial French and Japanese concepts were that the submarine should operate as a part of warfare in the littoral. Furthermore, the submarine force has been used to operating without constant communications with senior commanders; in a sense it has always had to operate within an established doctrine that governed their actions in the absence of communications. Since doctrine can be thought of as principles guiding actions in the absence of communications with one's seniors, perhaps this part of the naval Services can teach the others how it has managed to succeed at sea with doctrine so that other branches and combat arms need fear doctrine less.

Formal Navy doctrine suffered a setback with the introduction of new technologies and the end of the Anglo-Franco wars during the age of sail. Navy doctrine was developed and frequently refined during the wars between Britain and France over hundreds of years. During the age of sail, there were long periods of warfare with essentially the same technology--hence improvements to navy warfare came via other avenues of advancement. Additionally, modern recruitment techniques had yet to be discovered--hence improvements in personnel and leadership was not yet the way to improve combat potential. Advances in the naval art had to come in the area of doctrine. Debates over navy doctrine and the existence of written doctrine was normal practice. As navy doctrine advanced, so did combat potential.

Since the early part of the 19th century, two events have had a profound change effect on the nature of navy doctrine: technology and the frequency and participants of war itself. First, from the time of the introduction of the ironclad, navy technology has changed so fast and so often that navies have not had the time to deal with doctrinal issues for forces on hand. By the time of the Battle of Lissa (1866) between Italy and Austria, warship designs were advancing before navy doctrine could be re-evaluated and re-written. Navies turned more of their attention to dealing with improvements to naval art and combat potential by improvements in technologies, programming, rather than how to fight "smarter." More often than we would like to admit, new technologies have been introduced for which there was no accepted military doctrine for their use. Hence, improvements to combat potential increasingly came to be seen as the result of effective programming skills rather than skills in assessing warfighting doctrine. Today, we need to shift our focus to other, less expensive ways of improving combat potential, other than with the introduction of new technologies--in short, navy doctrine as a force builder.

Second, during the long wars between Britain and France, both sides fought their fleets in accordance with formal Navy doctrine. Each side sought improvements in their combat potential by improving <u>how</u> it fought relative to the other rather than by fielding new equipment. Once the wars between Britain and France ended, and the assumed adversary changed to other nations or no specific nation, the perceived need to refine the existing Navy doctrine was no longer critical.

A third factor may have also influenced the discouragement of open debate over doctrine in the U.S. Navy. Following their victories at Santiago, Rear Admirals William T. Sampson and Winfield Scott Schley, USN, engaged in public debates and discussions over their conduct during the Battle of Santiago (July 1898). Spanish Admiral Pascual Cervera had outmaneuvered the American North Atlantic Squadron and managed to enter the harbor at Santiago, Cuba, where he maintained a fleet-in-being. The Americans attempted to and eventually drew out the fleet as a result of joint actions taken ashore and at sea, resulting in a battle in which Cervera was defeated.[31] The public debate went on for years and necessitated a Presidential order for it to cease. Perhaps the acrimonious manner in which tactics were questioned poisoned the well in the U.S. Navy for subsequent frank and open debate and discussions of a doctrinal nature.

During the last decade of the Cold War, there was a renaissance in the U.S. concerning issues of how to fight--military doctrine. With the end of the Cold War, and the replacement of a single adversary with multiple or no specific adversary, it may be hard to sustain support for the armed forces as warfighting tools. If this happens, it may be hard to sustain development and revision of warfighting doctrine. If an enemy force has doctrine, it is more likely that one's own forces will study that doctrine and develop military doctrine of their own. If a potential enemy does not have doctrine, it might breed complacency in doctrinal development. On the other hand, Services with a long tradition of formal written doctrine and the supporting organizations, like the U.S. Army, will probably continue doctrinal development regardless of the nature of the threat.

A military must want good doctrine for it to have doctrine. Spain suffered navy doctrinal atrophy because its fleet was hardly engaged in combat after Trafalgar. A military must want to keep their military doctrine updated and be willing to fight to do this, otherwise it is easy to get sidetracked into only concern for programming. Good naval doctrine will come with the assignment of good personnel in doctrine development commands; hence the key, as usual, is in a reward structure that bestows promotion to those so detailed.

Pre-war doctrine cannot foresee all eventualities. No matter how well thought out military doctrine is before a war, it is very likely that forces will be used in a manner that has not been anticipated. When the real world does not develop as anticipated in the programmed world, navy forces will still go to sea, in the ships and aircraft that resulted from the fiscal realities that drove pre-war programming decisions. Doctrinal developments must even continue while a war is in progress.

There is a long history of warriors being adaptive and flexible using hardware designed for one type of combat in situations that were never envisaged by their designers. Such examples include the use of surfaced submarines attacking escorted convoys and "navalized" B-24 bombers used as long-range offensive interceptors against unarmed and lightly armed reconnaissance, transport, and other utility aircraft in the Pacific theater during World War II. When this happens, doctrine is generally created from the bottom-up but there is no reason that doctrinal innovators cannot adapt from similar circumstances faced by other forces.

Innovation in time of war is extremely difficult. Moreover, under today's concepts of short regional contingencies, will we have the time to innovate during the time span of future crises? The technological opportunities afforded by the development of the light-weight radial aircraft engine were capitalized upon by the U.S. Navy's inter-war peacetime doctrinal development for carrier warfare. It represented a missed opportunity for the Royal Navy. Great Britain's Navy, and the Fleet Air Arm suffered early in World War II because during the inter-war years, there was only modest activity within the Royal Navy to address changes in doctrine afforded by new aviation technologies. Doctrinal rigidity appears to have a marked negative influence on the appreciation of opportunities afforded by "revolutions in military affairs."[32]

Military doctrine should, and often must, be developed for situations not required by current policy or available resources. There is no reason that the military should not develop prototype military doctrine today for concepts of war under political and fiscal guidance different than that currently approved for programming purposes by governments which are presently in office. For example, France has issued a recent White Paper with five scenarios for programmatics involving future war. In addition, the French military has added a sixth scenario, not used in programmatics, for a re-emergent threat in Europe.[33]

Witness the restructuring of the American armed forces from being able to handle a European-centered global conventional war under President Ronald Reagan, to planned downsizing to handle only DESERT STORM-sized major regional contingencies and a program to reconstitute for global war under President George Bush, to a NATO alliance and a U.S. government that does not include plans to reconstitute a European-centered global conventional warfighting capability.[34] Before we lose the expertise on how we planned to fight and win a European-centered global conventional war, we might want to document it in formal written military doctrine so that if the doctrine is ever needed again, it will be available.

Before any war, there is an expected enemy against which military doctrine is designed. When the intelligence community has misrepresented the capabilities of the enemy, it is likely that prewar doctrine has suffered. For example, prior to World War II, Navy intelligence rated Japanese antisubmarine warfare capabilities much greater than subsequently demonstrated during the war. Paralleling this, the U.S. submarine force thought that its submarines were extremely vulnerable to fielded antisubmarine warfare weapons--again proven false under combat conditions. Put together, the submarine force developed a stealthy and cautious doctrine which had to be discarded upon analysis of combat lessons learned. Because of faulty pre-war threat assessments and associated doctrine, the submarine force had not extensively practiced for long combat patrols and they had not fully developed doctrine for the types of attacks (surfaced) which would become commonplace during the war.

Prewar theory has often been developed in a sterile non-political environment in which the "pure military" aspects of doctrine were stressed. It is impossible to separate the "pure military" aspects of warfare at the strategic and operational levels. Whereas the "pure military" solution might be to have an offensive and aggressive military doctrine, British

Vice Admiral Sir Edward Codrington learned at the Battle of Navarino (1827) that the resulting crushing defeat of the Turks so embarrassed the governments of Britain, France, and Russia that he had to be sacked and his career ruined. Yet Codrington's doctrine and fielded technology for the battle was virtually identical to that of the victorious Admiral Lord Horatio Nelson--but the political context was not. Codrington had learned only the lesson of Trafalgar and not Copenhagen.

It may be necessary to have different doctrines for different circumstances. During World War II, there was appropriately an offensive doctrine in the Royal Navy to deal with German surface raiders--an annihilation-oriented doctrine. Yet the navy doctrine to deal with subsurface raiders was correctly defensive and attrition-oriented. Similarly, military doctrine often prescribes some specific correlation of forces in one's favor prior to attack. The results of the Battle of the Coral Sea (1942) were, in part, a result of boldness and audacity on the part Rear Admiral Frank Jack Fletcher, USN, who ordered an attack with forces that were weaker than those of the enemy. Thus, military doctrine must allow for a preferred way of war with special considerations allowing for alternative courses of action. After all, there may be different geographic locations with different threats for which a single standing military doctrine is entirely inappropriate. In short, doctrine is a play book which should contain all the possible sanctioned plays which can be selected by the commander (tactics).

Doctrine and Change

Centralized military doctrine should not be cast in stone and must be subject to the interpretation of local commanders. Centralized doctrine must be supplemented with local instructions. The operator in the field must be allowed sufficient latitude to use military doctrine to his advantage and to supplement that doctrine with his own best judgment. Where doctrine is routinely supplemented or disregarded, then doctrine apparently needs to be adjusted. Inputs from the operators in the field are vital to ensuring that military doctrine does not become "doctrinaire." "For any military organization to remain doctrinally sound, it must be capable of questioning established principles and of synthesizing new ideas. When that ability is lost, the military force becomes a stagnant dinosaur, ready to be destroyed."[35] Defeat of the Japanese Navy in the Pacific during World War II can, in part, be attributed to their failure to learn and adapt their doctrine in the face of combat losses.[36]

Deviations from military doctrine, however, should not be the "right" of every officer in command. Indeed, a nation can only afford so many Nelsons before it would lack cohesion and suffer in combat capability. In general, the military should be expected to operate in accordance with their established doctrine. <u>Senior</u> commanders, however, must have the ability to deviate from established military doctrine when the conditions under which that doctrine was established no longer exist. Before deviating, one should be well-versed in established practices which provide the necessary background allowing such judgment. Like deviations from social etiquette, deviations from doctrine should be knowing rather than by chance. In the absence of changed circumstances, doctrine still represents the best way of doing the job and the way that one's seniors will assume that the job is done.[37]

Military doctrine will always be somewhat doctrinaire due to the inherent personality types attracted to senior government and military service.[38] The average army colonel or navy captain is, by his very nature, less perceptual than judgmental as well as more analytic than concerned with human issues. That will make he or she less likely to respond well to innovation which threatens to upset the established order and structure. Yet innovation in military doctrine is needed if we are to avoid the negative lessons of history. That would imply that psychological traits of military doctrine writers is at least as important as their tactical and combat experience, their education and training, and their rank.

The central issue of doctrine as "law" should take a book from the role of religious doctrine.[39] Even in the Catholic Church, "infallible" doctrine has generally been discussed and a consensus built prior to being formally issued. The Catholic Church has a hierarchy of doctrine, with a relatively modest amount of centralized "infallible" doctrine and regionally-adapted doctrine more subject to interpretation. Similarly, doctrine in the Catholic Church is provided with the illusion of permanence because of the long time period associated with change. Change does occur in Church doctrine, but over long periods of time. On the other hand, despite the illusion of permanence and "infallible" doctrine, the Church recognizes the need for and allows doctrinal change.

Another way to look at the question of interpretation of doctrine is to recognize that if two symphony orchestras with two different conductors attempt to both play the same musical score, they will undoubtedly sound different to the trained observer. Both performances will present the program advertised by the symphony, but the relative success of each effort will depend upon a variety of external factors (such as quality of instruments) as well as the interpretation of the musical score by the conductor. Doctrine cannot be cast in stone any more than can be Beethovan's greatest symphonies.

Military doctrine has changed due to a variety of circumstances. The circumstances have ranged from Acts of Parliament and Congress, to lessons learned in battle, to changes in types of governments. For example, when types of government change, or otherwise a purge of the officer corps occurs, it has often taken a long time for the new officers to develop their own expertise in warfare and their own doctrine. Officers from the old regime are often trapped in doctrinal thought that is no longer appropriate--as were Southern army officers during the American civil war.

The political realities that face a navy obviously have an effect on the types of military doctrine that can be developed. A number of countries have made drastic changes in forms of government during which all previous military doctrine was automatically considered obsolete. The lesson here is that military doctrine must transcend politics, although it obviously is subservient to it. Both the French and Soviet Navies after their respective revolutions suffered greatly due to the loss of expertise from the experts in navy warfare tainted by the previous regime. On the other hand, a change in type of government, such as in France during and after World War II, led to an instantaneous change in navy doctrine. The growth and professionalization of the Royal Navy can be traced back to the introduction of army officers as seagoing generals who built on and improved existing royalist fighting doctrine. In short, if creating doctrine "from scratch," build upon existing doctrine rather than re-inventing the wheel.

Perhaps the most significant reasons that military doctrine has changed, however, have been changes in the international security environment which have had a profound effect on policy, available resources, strategies and campaign concepts, threats, and emerging technology. A good example of this is the effect made on Japan by the arrival of Commodore Matthew C. Perry, USN. Perry shocked the Shogunal officials into recognizing the extreme vulnerability of Japan resulting in a major naval building program, doctrinal renaissance, and the capability to fight the United States at sea.[40] With the simultaneous change in policies, resources, strategies, threats, technologies, etc., going on today, there ought to be a doctrinal renaissance in the various armed forces of the world. From the lessons of the history of doctrinal development, it would appear that doctrinal innovation, like other forms of innovation in the military, is not a linear process.

Military doctrine must be developed from the tried and true lessons of history, but also with an eye toward the opportunities presented by emerging technologies and new political realities. History is important to learn what has been tried. It is not, however, a total guide to how we must fight in the future. One of the lessons of history is to learn how often a new technology has been introduced without a commensurate parallel advancement in doctrine. Changes in government will also present new opportunities for improved tactics, operational art, and strategy.[41]

Technological innovation during war is the type of originality that is necessary to support our naval forces. Technological innovation, however, has not always resulted in parallel doctrinal developments, indicating a need to formalize this process. This inability to adapt to new technologies is as true at sea as it has always been ashore--the failure of knights to adapt to the firearm being the classic case in point.[42] Simply put, there have been too many opportunities lost when technologies have been available or even introduced but military doctrine lagged behind.

Improved military doctrine does not need to have a technological push/pull. Improved combat potential can be had by improving how to fight with existing capabilities. When the firearm did not initially reform how war was fought ashore, improvements to infantry tactical formations were discovered to be the solution to how to overcome the mounted knight and would have yielded the same result even without the invention of the firearm.[43] Similarly, doctrinal innovation can take place in the absence of technological advances. This is what happened with Marine Corps amphibious doctrine--conceptually developed in 1921--with the subsequent "borrowing" of Japanese landing craft technology not occurring until just prior to World War II.[44]

There are other good Asian cases to consider. By the mid-1930s, the Imperial Japanese Navy recognized that despite all of the technological and industrial efforts being made to upgrade the fleet, their projected capabilities would not result in a force capable of meeting the improving U.S. Navy in a decisive battle at sea. The Imperial Japanese Navy, therefore, gave more impetus to the development of night tactics and eventually formed specialized night combat groupings (*yasengun*) that would weaken the U.S. Pacific Fleet to such a degree that the subsequent daylight battle between main fleets would be a foregone conclusion. Thus a threat was met with a doctrinal and not technological solution.[45]

It is **not easy to institute a significant doctrinal change** in large organizations. The legacy of the difficulty to change within the Royal Navy alone leads one to conclude that doctrinal change is akin to religious or ideological war. The shift of the fleet's center of gravity from the battleship to the aircraft carrier in the U.S. Navy was a consequence of both the actions at Pearl Harbor and the controversial doctrinal development undertaken by a small group of heretical officers within the U.S. Navy throughout the 1930s.[46] Similarly, alternatives to approved fleet doctrine for submarine operations had been developed off-line, making it easier to change the tasking for Pacific Fleet submarines at the beginning of the war.[47] Changes to doctrine in the British and American navies were the result of sequential bureaucratic operations--attrition warfare, not one decisive battle--annihilation warfare. For those who want to make major changes to a navy, it would be wise to plan a bureaucratic campaign with the goal of "getting the camel's nose under the tent."

To foster innovation in the face of standing doctrine, navies probably need formal structures where new ideas are tested. These organizations already exist in the form of centers of excellence, such as: the Navy Strike Warfare Center, the Navy Fighter Weapons School, the Surface Warfare Development Group, Submarine Development Squadron TWELVE and the Atlantic and Pacific Fleet Tactical Training Groups. Hence, all that would need to be done is to formalize lines of communications with those and similar organizations, with an eye toward Navy doctrine development. Indeed, there is a long history in many navies of the world of having squadrons of evolution, or other named units, whose function was to test new doctrine. This concept was advanced by Rear Admiral Stephen B. Luce, USN, with regard to the role of the Naval War College and the U.S. North Atlantic Squadron.[48] Historical test and development units were more singularly focused on operational doctrinal development rather than today's units which often spend a significant amount of their effort in support of programming.

We must be prepared to change military doctrine during a war itself. If we do not accept the possibility of doctrinal change during a war, then we risk dooming warriors to rigid adherence to doctrine despite the lessons learned during the initial stages of war. Nelson learned to adapt during war and succeeded. Codrington did not adapt and failed in his mission although he succeeded tactically. Rear Admiral Sir Christopher Craddock failed to adapt at the Battle of Coronel (1914) and was defeated. The history of doctrinal change by the U.S. submarine force during the initial stages of World War II in the Pacific is extremely instructive. Changing military doctrine during a war can be exceedingly difficult. On the other hand, the lessons of the German army during the latter stages of World War I demonstrate that a living and breathing system of military doctrine can make successful adaptation during combat easier to accomplish.[49]

When doctrine is stagnant, there have been disastrous consequences. For example, on December 10, 1941, the Singapore-based *Force Z* of the Royal Navy was attacked by Japanese aircraft with the resulting loss of the battleships *HMS Prince of Wales* and *HMS Repulse*.[50] The force commander, Admiral Sir Thomas Phillips, RN, elected to operate outside of the umbrella of the Royal Air Force and his own carrier, *HMS Indomitable*, was still aground in Jamaica. The lack of defensive air cover is generally given as the reason for the loss of these two battleships. Yet, when *HMS Ark Royal* was previously attacked by German fighters in the European theater of the war, her fighters were kept below so that antiaircraft fire would be unimpeded--in accordance with existing doctrine which was proven later to be inadequate.[51] Hence Admiral Phillips may not have known that antiaircraft fire was insufficient to defend himself against air attack. Doctrine should have provided Phillips with some alternatives, such as remaining in port as a fleet-in-being or withdrawal and consolidation with other allied forces, other than to simply sortie from Singapore and attempt an attack on enemy transports landing troops on the Malay Peninsula.

The difficulty in changing doctrine can be best studied with detailed and fully developed case studies that result in specific lessons learned. For example, Stephen Rosen's *Winning the Next War: Innovation and the Modern Military* is an excellent book written about change in military organizations.[52] This book has a number of cases which provide the military doctrine supervisor with a quick overview of the problems of change during peacetime, during war, etc. To really get into the heart of the doctrinal change, single book-length case studies need to be also consulted. After studying such in depth cases, one can more easily accept the need for recommendations contained therein, such as: support at the top, a mechanism for the building of consensus, and an organizational climate that accepts rational analysis as the basis for doctrine.[53]

The experiences of Spanish Vice Admiral José de Mazarredo Salazar strongly suggest that just having the good idea is simply not enough. De Mazarredo was the author of excellent doctrinal works and many good recommendations for improvement of the Spanish fleet prior to the defeat at Trafalgar. Although de Mazarredo was never defeated at sea, and thus had the credibility of a proven warrior, his outspoken criticism of the state of the fleet, and its lack of combat preparedness, as well as his audacity in questioning Spanish foreign policy, doomed all of his good ideas to the history books and not as any actual improvement for the Spanish Navy.[54]

It appears **naval doctrine is easier to change when it is written**. Japan did not begin to develop formal centralized written doctrine until 1887, within years of the formation of the first modern fleet. The first formal Battle Instructions (*Kaisen yômurei*) were issued in 1901. They were revised five times before World War II and were paralleled by a number of subordinate and parallel doctrines for amphibious and naval air combat.[55] During the war, the

Japanese were able to successfully change their basic battle doctrine from being centered around the battleship to being centered around the aircraft carrier.

When doctrine is written, it is a target that can be identified and defeated by adept bureaucratic maneuver or firepower. When the target is a belief, it is internalized and more difficult to root out. The U.S. Marine Corps was unable to embrace the concept of amphibious warfare until an enlightened Commandant retired senior officers opposed to its introduction. The French Navy was unable to get past the *jeune école* until supporting flag officers were retired. Left over Cold Warriors may need to be similarly disposed of in order to advance from open-ocean warfare to warfare along the littoral.

Yet even when naval doctrine is written, it may be difficult to change. For example, the fundamental policies contained in the naval white paper *...From the Sea*[56] remain sound even a few years following its issuance. This document serves as the basis of current naval doctrine. The basic and fundamental guidelines contained in this white paper would only be revised if there were major and fundamental changes in the perceived threat, available resources, or governmental goals--all of which are not likely to change. For example, has there reemerged a resurgent global threat causing a fundamental revision to the nation's regionally-focused military strategy? Or, have the resources been reduced enough to preclude participation in major regional contingencies other than as an equal player with other nations. Or, has the American public failed to embrace the role of world "fireman" and is the message from the home from to return to isolationism?

Each of these fundamental and basic issues would require a revision to the white paper *...From the Sea*. Yet a revision to this white paper was needed in order to more fully develop some concepts of interest today, such as naval presence, and to reflect the personal views of new naval and political leaders. Without a change to these three fundamental issues of threat, resources, or goals, the basic philosophy behind *...From the Sea* remained the same and the newly issued *Forward...From the Sea* only made improvements on the margin.[57] Hence, any new naval doctrine issued subsequent to *Forward...From the Sea* will largely be consistent with the original *...From the Sea* and naval doctrine prepared prior to that time.

Military doctrine should be the province of the warrior. However, as heretical as it may sound, doctrinal <u>innovation</u> probably depends more upon one's administrative skills than warfighting skills. Obviously more than an appreciation of warfighting must be had by the administrative innovator, but history provides us with many examples of skilled warriors who have served their nations well in times of extreme stress who have won the war but been unable to articulate how they did what they did in a manner that it would successfully change military doctrine. A wise navy will create a system by which it can extract the doctrinal lessons learned from its proven combat leaders so that innovation in formal doctrine will follow. On the other hand, there is no strong evidence that excellent writers of doctrine automatically make good combat leaders. Complete doctrinal development and revision needs the participation of both warriors and bureaucrats.

Doctrinal innovation will benefit with the creation of formal organizations charged with monitoring doctrine. Without such organizations, who takes responsibility for the fostering of new good ideas? When the aircraft was introduced into the U.S. Navy, farseeing officers with vision understood the need for an organization, the Bureau of Aeronautics, that would be responsible for the future development of the new idea. The Royal Navy had no such organization and thus was deficient in its development of the concepts for fleet combat centered on the aircraft.[58]

Above all, for military doctrine to be a living and breathing document, it needs to be supported by informal and unofficial organizations which support the non-doctrinaire writings of officers with a new idea. No matter how important the influx of new ideas from outside of the normal system, it is more often the case that the insiders will need to carry the ball in order that military doctrine change. Significant change due to external direction, such as Congress, has been done but should not be the norm. A profession can not be a profession unless it can reform and regulate itself.

<u>Preparing Military Doctrine</u>

Measures of effectiveness (MOEs) are needed for doctrine. The existence of a written doctrine is no more the "proof" that it is acceptable than the existence of an arms control treaty is "proof" of the effective control of arms. Some of the MOEs for military doctrine should be: (1), success in combat; (2), acceptability by the navy and the nation; (3), adaptability and flexibility in the face of external and internal change; (4), consistency with the lessons of history; (5), relevancy to the most likely scenarios; and (6), attainability in the face of resource restraints. At the heart of effective doctrine is a sound training and education program. Without training, doctrine is unfulfilled wishes of how one would like to operate.

Armed with good MOEs, one needs to design a cybernetic-like feedback system to monitor naval doctrine in the fleet and to feed back the necessary changes resulting from actual operational practice. Feedback should not only come via informal monitoring of the product, but also via formal inputs from training sites and commands responsible for exercises and evaluations. The Catholic Church has a built-in feedback system, in the form of the confessional, which allows the virtual immediate measurement of how much of its doctrine is being followed on a day-to-day basis. The message to internalize is simply that if the MOE for military doctrine is merely that it is published, it runs the risk of either becoming doctrinaire or irrelevant, neither of which is acceptable.

There will be separate MOEs for military doctrine in support of warfighting commanders and doctrine in support of programming. Military doctrine can support both of these, but the doctrine itself may not be the same--e.g. there was one U.S. operational doctrine for the deterrence and fighting of the nuclear phase of war in the mid-1980s while simultaneously there was a separate programming doctrine for deterrence and nuclear warfighting in support of the Strategic Defense Initiative (SDI). Although doctrine in support of programming is important and may eventually change actual operational military doctrine if a program is fielded and the systems work as theorized, the true MOE for programming doctrine is the success of the program and not necessarily success in combat. Doctrine for fielded combat forces must be based upon observed actual capability of weapons systems in as close as possible to a realistic combat environment.

MOEs for military doctrine may not necessarily be universal--indeed they may be culturally biased. In the Soviet Union, doctrinal development started at the top with policy and strategy with subordinate military doctrinal (operational art) and operational concepts flowing downward. Adherence to military strategy and doctrine (operational art) was, in part, a method to demonstrate unity of effort. In the U.S., military doctrine has more often started with the development of a new technology or battlefield success and the subsequent need to codify doctrine.[59] Adherence to a military doctrine is often a demonstration of the strength of informal networks and formal organizations.

Successful navy doctrine has been prepared by a variety of individuals both inside and outside of the sea Services. Doctrine has been written by navy officers of all ranks (admirals to lieutenant), civilians (including Jesuit priests) working for navies, retired officers, army officers, legislatures, and even bright landlubbers who have never gone to sea and never faced the cold steel of an enemy. The tension between the administrative officers (the *plume*) and the warriors (the *épée*) found in the French Navy during the age of sail is paralleled today by questions of who should write doctrine for modern navies. A successful coach in sports can devise masterful playbooks that he himself cannot carry out. In the hands of talented athletes, however, this playbook can yield victory on the field of contest.[60]

Although doctrine must eventually be accepted by the profession that adopts it, the professionals themselves do not necessarily need to be the authors of that doctrine. Indeed, history more often documents successful written navy doctrine being prepared by other than serving officers than by that group themselves. On the other hand, informal, unwritten, and decentralized doctrine in navies has most often been developed by serving officers themselves who have had the benefit of formal education and training in their profession and the years of operational hands-on experience that no landlubber can bring to the table.

In addition to the tension between the pen and the sword, there has been another consistent theme of tension in the history of navy and naval doctrine--control vs. independence. Navy doctrine began in Spain, England, and France as an attempt to ensure the massing of firepower with the cannon; a control solution to the disorder of the battle at sea. Without advances in technology, doctrinal innovation was often the method of advancement in combat potential. Against a second-rate enemy, commanders learned that they could afford to depart from the battle line and take the fight to the enemy. With advances in technologies, certain types of navy assets were fought by officers that also fostered the idea of independence and innovation in battle rather than control. Fleet commanders need to know when to insist on control rather than independence--there are times for both. Perhaps the relative degree of independence afforded navies helps explain the lack of a modern tradition of written doctrinal debate.

The role of independent thought in doctrinal development is central to a healthy process. This suggests a role for selected retired officers. For example, when General Maxwell Thurman, USA, needed to develop the military doctrine for corps commanders, the work of the general officer, he realized that he could not rely upon the staff action officer to write such doctrine since they had never been a general officer in command of a corps. As head of the Army's TRADOC, Thurman hired a group of retired corps commanders to prepare the first draft of the new doctrine.[61]

One of the key lessons from healthy doctrinal development history is that military doctrine writers need to be innovative and unconstrained by the current view of how to fight. Finding officers with such vision is difficult but not impossible. The officer who first developed American concepts and doctrine for amphibious warfare was Major Earl H. Ellis, USMC. The first American to understand that the striking power of aircraft at sea could equal that of the battleship was Lieutenant Commander Henry C. Mustin, USN. Both of these officers, however, needed senior general and flag officers within the established organization to protect these new ideas and allow them to grow.[62]

Military doctrine for nuclear warfare is an interesting anomaly. Despite the tremendous increase in the potential firepower of fleets with the introduction of nuclear weapons, navies generally abdicated their responsibilities for the preparation of nuclear warfighting doctrine; allowing civilian academics and analysts to prepare what can only be described as theories of how to fight a nuclear war. Military officers eventually translated those theories into practical war plans and targeting orders, but the debate over doctrine was largely done outside of the military and with the full and routine participation of legislatures.

The participation of civilians in nuclear, and navy nuclear, warfighting doctrine was primarily true regarding strikes against the shore and to a lesser degree in fleet versus fleet. In general, the theories of nuclear warfare were developed by special academic theorists who benefited from the premise that nuclear war was irrational and/or the end of politics. Rather than seeing nuclear weapons as just another weapon with a larger bang, they were placed into a category with direct civilian oversight and navies were left with generally preparing programs to field the weapons systems and operate them safely and over the technical details of targeting. With some exceptions, great doctrinal debates over the conduct of nuclear war from or at sea were generally left to those outside the naval Services.

The mechanics of the doctrinal development process are collections of inputs to and influences on doctrine, actual formulation of doctrine, and finally dissemination.[63] Existing organizations with a history of doctrinal development are generally strongest in the formulation phase and weak in the other two. The U.S. Army has an extremely strong program of letting doctrinal ideas appear first as articles subject to debate and revision. Such a program tends to make the operational forces more of a participant in the process than if they simply received revised versions of new field manuals.

Doctrine must be meaningful and address tough substantial issues. If doctrine is allowed to become superficial, it will become irrelevant. If it deals with important issues, it is bound to be controversial eventually as someone has another idea. The objective in doctrinal development is not consensus but rather reflection, introspection, analysis, and preparation of a menu of recommendations from which the combat commander can select his tactics. A natural tendency of any bureaucracy is to avoid confrontation; hence stifle change. Doctrinal development must welcome recommendations for change.

As a series of examples of what are meaningful issues that should be contained in doctrinal publications, the author offers the following suggestions. What is the principal style of warfare--firepower, maneuver, or protection? Is the principal form of warfare offensive or defensive? Is warfare annihilation or attrition-based? What is the objective of a fleet engagement--sinking or demobilizing the enemy, taking the enemy prize, or mission kill? Should the object of an attack be the enemy's transports/auxiliaries or its convoy escorts? When attacking, should some portion of the force be held in reserve? When defending an amphibious objective area or a convoyed force, should the defending fighting force attempt to engage the enemy attacking force by seeking him out or by lying in wait on the defensive? What are the proper command and control relationships in the joint littoral? Do all naval forces operate in task type organizations? Are allies or ad hoc coalition partners fully integrated with own forces or assigned a separate area of operations? How far should the combat commander on the scene comply with doctrine issued by bureaucracies ashore? How much should the commander rely upon enemy intentions versus capabilities?

The Future of Military Doctrine

Joint doctrine and multinational doctrine become more important as national forces downsize. As militaries around the world are downsizing, due to the new international security environment, they have to fight smarter as smaller forces. Jointness, alliances and ad hoc coalitions are the logical steps that governments will take to ensure that their national objectives are met with smaller national military forces. As military Services, who have been used to operating under their own semi-independent doctrine, are forced to operate routinely with other Services, it is more important that they all understand how the other thinks and intends to act. The Royal Navy has successfully adapted to all of these new conditions.

Many medium and smaller-sized navies in the world look forward to the frequent multinational training opportunities afforded by deployments of U.S. naval forces to their home waters. If the U.S. government wishes the benefit of continued forward deployment of our naval forces and foreign navies intend to operate with the U.S. Navy in the future, they are going to have to become well-versed in our new written doctrine. This, in turn, implies that U.S. Navy doctrine must be developed from the perspective of the need to share that doctrine with foreign navies.

Multinational doctrine for navy forces will be inherently different than multinational doctrine for land forces. When navy forces operate in an international context, they retain their sovereignty and are quickly able to revert to national control. Hence, governments do in fact exercise a great deal of national control over navy forces even if those forces are operating in a multinational environment. On the other hand, when a nation contributes ground forces to a multinational effort, the forces tend to be mixed and eventually commanded by officers from other countries. The ground forces are not generally subject to the same degree of residual control by their parent nations. Hence, multinational doctrine for ground forces appears to be a <u>vital</u> necessity whereas multinational doctrine for navy forces can be far less inclusive with national military doctrine filling in the voids.

The fundamental unit for navies is the ship, which generally operates as part of a task group with a flag officer in command. Commanding officers of individual ships have a good deal of operational at-sea experience before being entrusted to command. Even if a ship is detached on peacekeeping duties, it is generally an integral part of a task group under the command of and in constant communication with a flag officer. On the other hand, the fundamental unit for ground forces is the battalion, commanded by officers with generally less operational experience in the field than the comparable sea-going officer. Ground units less that battalion size commanded by junior officers are often employed as part of multinational peacekeeping forces. Ground forces simply have needed formal doctrine of all types to guide these more junior officers and non-commissioned officers more than have ships with senior officers in command. This is not to argue that navies are unique; but they are rather different, thus further explaining why navies have not recently always embraced written and formal navy doctrine.[64] On the other hand, the very first written navy doctrine, from the year 1270 when the embryonic Spanish Navy was still an integral part of the army, presented the case that war at sea was fundamentally different than war ashore.

There may be a parallel in history to the role that navy and aviation officers play in combat as a whole. During the middle ages, the foot soldier gradually lost his ability to fight as a cohesive unit and was upstaged by the man on horseback.[65] In this era, sometimes fifty percent of a formation was formed by men on horseback. Normally, individual men are insignificant units on the field of battle, unless they are a part of a tactical unit--infantry in the case of foot soldiers. With the creation of the knight on horseback, this relationship of fighting men to tactical units became temporarily displaced. Knights were initially incapable of being formed into tactical units. The best of men aspired to be knights who fought individually and generally under a far lesser degree of control by the commander. Eventually men on horseback later were formed into tactical units--cavalry and were subjected to a bit more control.

Perhaps it would be instructive to study the similarity of the knight on horseback to aerial dogfight and to the *mêlée* of the days of sail. In each case, there appear to be forces that attempt to control the engagement debating those who would simply wade in and defeat the enemy. In each case, doctrine was needed, but that doctrine would be fundamentally different than the doctrine for the infantry formation, the strategic bomber, or the defense of convoys.

The differences between doctrinal development in the French Navy and Army suggest the need for similar comparisons between ground and sea Services in other countries.[66] Such comparisons would probably allow for some inputs to and influences on military doctrine to be the same allowing for judgment as to why different doctrines might develop in different Services or how the doctrine for one Service might influence another.

A nation with military responsibilities that extend over a wide geographic area can have **more than one military doctrine**. Obviously any nation that has global responsibilities will have a core military doctrine, but the requirements to service very different threats in vastly dissimilar geographic locations and peoples of disparate strategic cultures may mean that it will be proper to have slightly diverse doctrines for different geographic areas. The way of war in Southwest Asia (SWA) may simply not be applicable in the Korean peninsula, even if both are categorized as major regional contingencies.[67] Similarly, we should expect to see significant differences in Russian operational art [military doctrine] in their Western Theater of Military Operations (WTVD) against an "enemy" with technological superiority and in their Southern TVD where they themselves may have technological superiority.[68] There have often been sound reasons why the operational and tactical doctrine found in the U.S. Atlantic and Pacific Fleets has been different. It may prove hard to centralize them.

Perhaps we should recognize that there is a need for different military doctrine at different levels of warfare. For example, history tells us of many examples of defensive strategies and defensive doctrines with aggressive offensive doctrine emphasizing *élan* at the tactical-level of warfare.[69] It may be necessary to ensure that the offensive fighting spirit at the tactical-level is not meant to spill over into the operational and strategic levels of warfare. If that is the case, it reinforces the need for flag and general officers to understand the differences between the tactical-level doctrine taught to the individual sailor, marine, airman, or soldier and the doctrine that governs his personal activities.

Overreliance on offensive doctrine is, in part, directly attributable to the defeat of the Japanese Navy in the Pacific during World War II.[70] At the Battle of the Coral Sea (1942), the Japanese striking force attempted to seek out the allied battle fleet instead of remaining with its own transports in a defensive posture. Pre-war Japanese Navy doctrine had not completed a concept for defense of their carrier battle forces, let alone the transports, in any other manner than an offensive strike against the enemy. Admiral Raymond A. Spruance USN saw the virtue of the defensive and operated initially in a defensive posture at the Battle of the Philippine Sea (1944) resulting in a major American victory.

The offensive and quick annihilation warfare are not always the correct answer--defense and long-term attrition warfare are often the appropriate measures.[71] The original philosophy underlying the concepts of modern "maneuver" warfare comes from China and the days of Julius Caesar. The U.S. Marine Corps has embraced the concepts of Sun Tzu contained in

The Art of War, written around 400 B.C.[72] Indeed, in their capstone Service-unique doctrinal publication, *Warfighting*, FMFM-1, Sun Tzu is quoted at the beginning of the chapter on "The Theory of War:"[73]

> "Invincibility lies in the defense;
> the possibility of victory in the attack.
> One defends when his strength is inadequate;
> he attacks when it is abundant."

A further understanding of the value of the defense can be found in other classical Chinese literature, such as: the *Ssu-ma Fa*, the *Wu-tzu*, the *Wei Liao-tzu*, the T'ai Kung's *Six Secret Teachings*, the *Three Strategies* of Huang Shih-kung, and the medieval *Questions and Replies* between T'and T'ai-tsung and Li Wei-kung.[74] Another Chinese classic, Lao Tzu's *Tao Te Ching* (*The Book of the Way*), which predates Sun Tzu by a few hundred years, teaches that:

> "When two great forces oppose each other,
> the victory will go
> to the one that knows how to yield."[75]

The influence of Sun Tzu and other ancient Chinese philosophers on navy warfare has not been well explored in the West. The Imperial Japanese Navy made a thorough study of such "maneuver" warfare doctrine and embraced it prior to World War I, about the same time as they formulated their initial war plans against the U.S. One scholar has argued that it was because the Japanese failed to remember the teachings of Sun Tzu and instead became fascinated by German models that they prepared poorly for war with America.[76]

The subjects of warfare by rapid annihilation and long-term attrition warfare, and the offense and defense are critical questions and issues for doctrinal development.[77] Whereas the Chinese ground forces doctrine may currently be generally biased toward long-term attrition warfare and the defense, ancient Chinese doctrine was oriented toward "maneuver" warfare and subduing the enemy without actually engaging him--due to then-particular geographic and demographic conditions. This does not mean that modern Western military nations need to follow such ancient teachings given their different conditions and role in the world. What is necessary, however, is a thorough understanding of the culture of potential enemies so that we can correctly predict and interpret their military and naval doctrine. Simply put, there is no one universally correct military doctrine.

The first division of warfare into annihilation and attrition was by Raimondo Montecuccoli, an Italian lieutenant general and field marshal in the army of the Austrian Hapsburgs in the 17th Century.[78] Montecuccoli's writings were accepted by Frederick the Great. Reportedly Clausewitz also accepted this bifurcation and was in the middle of revising *Vom Krieg* to encompass the theory when he died.

The first real acceptance of these theories in actual combat was by Helmuth von Moltke and Alfred von Schlieffen.[79] While Chief of Staff, Moltke developed the concept of the continuous strategic-operational sequence which would defeat the enemy in one great and decisive battle of annihilation--the *vernichtungs* or *kesselschlact*--rather than the standard attrition warfare of the day. Schlieffen further refined the concept of the rapid decisive campaign in his warfare of annihilation, or *vernichtungsschlact*.

The concept of annihilation and attrition as two opposite poles was further refined by the German historian Hans Delbrück, who termed the two types of warfare *niederwerfungsstrategie* (annihilation) and *ermattungsstrategie* (exhaustion).[80] The most complete treatment of the two concepts is to be found in the post-World War I lectures and writings of General and Professor Aleksandr A. Svechin.[81] His book *Strategy* was essentially devoted to advocating attrition war over that which he termed "destruction." Svechin wrote probably the most exhaustive treatise of the two different types of warfare with numerous historical examples.[82]

In annihilation warfare, victory follows a decisive engagement against the center of gravity--the enemy fleet. Warfare of annihilation was the basic strategy (War Plan Orange) developed by the U.S. Navy and Army for war in the Pacific prior to World War II. This form of warfare subordinates all actions to a single supreme purpose. Under annihilation, withdrawal is normally not considered an honorable alternative. Warfare by annihilation ashore has been successfully practiced by few commanders--Alexander the Great, Hannibal, Julius Caesar, and Napoleon Bonaparte--but has been an accepted way of war at sea.

With an annihilation doctrine, there must be a subordinate doctrine for an exploitation phase. If the objective of a battle or an engagement is the total annihilation of the enemy force, then the victorious commander has to have an established doctrine about how far he will exploit his victory. This issue has come back to haunt many commanders over history-- each being criticized during his lifetime, and in history, for not having fully exploited the immediate victory with subsequent destruction of the enemy force as it left the battle space.

French Admiral Anne-Hilarion de Costentin, Comte de Tourville and a proven charismatic combat commander, failed to exploit a major victory against the combined English and Dutch fleets at Bévéziers [Beachy Head] (1690). British Admiral Lord George Brydges Rodney failed to exploit his victory at the Battle of the Saints (1782) and the innovative Admiral Lord Richard Howe did the same at the Glorious First of June (1789). Japanese Admiral Itô Yûkô achieved a decisive victory over China at the Battle of the Yalu [Yellow Sea] (1894) and was severely criticized for not exploiting the victory--thus allowing an enemy fleet-in-being to remain.

There were a few very notable examples of failure to exploit the battlefield victory during World War II. Admiral Mikawa Gun'ichi's failure to exploit his victory after the Battle off Savo Island (August 1942) was, in part, due to a failure in doctrine.[83] Of course Admiral Raymond Spruance's decision to remain and protect the invasion force instead of exploiting his victory at the Battle of the Philippine Sea (June 1944) led, in part, to the decision by Admiral William Halsey, at the Battle of Leyte Gulf (October 1944) to not stay with the invasion force but instead seek out the enemy's carriers. In short, if one's end state is to annihilate an enemy surface fleet, it must be done ruthlessly and included in doctrine. Victory may be determined by who leaves the battlefield in retreat, but the desired end state can go beyond this intermediate concept.

During the Thirty Years War (1618-1648), in which France became the dominant power on the continent of Europe, French Marshal Henri de la Tour d'Auvergne, Vicomte de Turenne, achieved the withdrawal of Holy Roman Empire forces from a city but then he chose to not exploit this immediate success with a pursuit and annihilation of the enemy. In a subsequent encounter in 1674, Turenne maneuvered Austrian General Count Raimondo Montecuccoli and William Frederick, the Great Elector of Brandenburg, out of Alsace without engaging them in battle.[84] Montecuccoli had demonstrated his own "maneuver" successes against Turenne in 1673 and 1675. In his writings, Clausewitz expresses his destain for generals who sought to attain a decision without battle.[85] Some of the traditions of ground-based "maneuver" warfare clearly include not engaging the enemy unless it is required. If navies are to adopt "maneuver" warfare doctrine, then they are going to have to come to grips with subordinate doctrine outlining policies for the opportunities of the exploitation phase of annihilation warfare.

The navy counterpart to attrition warfare is *guerre de course*. Examples include convoy defense practiced in the World War II Battle of the Atlantic and other forms of warfare where one single engagement or battle is not crucial to the outcome. Despite the plan to fight a war of annihilation in the Pacific during World War II, Admiral William Halsey, actually engaged in a war of attrition against the Japanese--although he was continually seeking a decisive battle of annihilation.[86] Attrition warfare is realistic under today's environment and allows the commander a higher degree of flexibility. Under attrition, withdrawal is regularly considered an honorable alternative. Warfare ashore by attrition has been successfully practiced by many more commanders--Pericles during the Peloponesian Wars, Frederick the Great in the Seven Years' War,[87] Britain during the World War II air defense Battle of Britain, and by the Russians in their Second Great Patriotic War.

The obvious question is what then to do about this concept of "maneuver" warfare. "Maneuver" warfare is a philosophy of warfare that can serve to support either warfare of annihilation or warfare of attrition. Since modern naval warfare will still embrace aspects of annihilation and attrition warfare, it will need to focus on the contributions that can be made by "maneuver" warfare to both.[88] The greatest problem with the concept of "maneuver" warfare doctrine in the United States is that most native speakers of American-English assume that they know what the concept means because they recognize the word "maneuver." In fact, the concept of "maneuver" warfare doctrine, as articulated by the U.S. Marine Corps and the U.S. Army, is far more complex than "movement," suggesting that perhaps the use of the term *manoeuvre*, in French, would force both the writer and reader of doctrine to recognize the difference. Indeed, a review of French Navy doctrinal literature reveals a wealth of conceptual ideas about *manoeuvre* warfare doctrine for navies.[89]

A major lesson to be learned from the doctrine of the Imperial Japanese Navy was that early in-depth analysis and doctrinal concept development was to give way to sloganeering and the use of catchy phrases which were not subject to criticism. As purely Japanese Navy doctrine emerged after the Sino-Japanese War and matured throughout the years prior to World War II, a series of phrases found their way into most official pronouncements and policy directives, such as "using a few to conquer many" (*ka o motte, shû i seu-su*) and "fight the enemy on sight" (*kenteki hissen*). This mystical approach to naval doctrine did not serve the Imperial Japanese Navy well.[90]

A **doctrinal renaissance**, necessitated by the need to explain to others how we think and intend to act, is a major opportunity to educate army and air force officers in the profession of arms by the naval Services. Formal training and education, exercises, exchange tours of duty, etc., represent excellent opportunities to educate these officers in the naval way of warfare. Since we will all be cooperating with each other more than we ever have, it is vitally important that we train and educate them correctly. The better our peacetime doctrinal development, the more likely that we will be able to succeed when it comes time to act. Doctrinal development complemented by training, education, and exercises, are ways to reduce risk of poor operations in the more complex joint and multinational international security environment.

Although navies will eventually have to develop doctrine for all types of operations, they should give priority to that which will ease the transition from informal customary unwritten to formal written doctrine. If a navy wishes to develop warfighting doctrine first, even though it will actually be engaged in immediate military operations other than war, then develop the warfighting doctrine first. The transition to formal written doctrine will be difficult, but not impossible, and each Service should be allowed to make the choice themselves what will be developed first.

Similarly, one might argue that there will never be an independent land, air, or naval campaign in the future. Even if such predictions are true, it may be easier for navies to enter the world of formal written doctrine by first analyzing and preparing doctrine for the independent naval campaign by using historical examples and theorizing for the future. From the building blocks of Service-unique and multi-Service doctrine will come good joint and multinational doctrine.

The U.S. Navy and Marine Corps have now published their initial centralized multi-Service doctrinal publication, *Naval Warfare*, NDP-1.[91] This document serves as an overview and introduction to the more substantive follow-on doctrinal publications which will address naval intelligence, operations, logistics, planning, and command and control. Of note is the naval Services embracing of the three levels of warfare, the concepts of center of gravity and critical vulnerability, and the principles of war--none of which are doctrine but all of which are major statements of policy.

Naval Warfare establishes that naval forces will be task organized and will favor offensive and "maneuver" warfare. It reviews the historical and current roles, missions, and functions of the naval Services and highlights inherent operational capabilities emphasized under current conditions. *Naval Warfare* also commits the naval Services to full partnership in joint and multinational operations.

There has been a great deal of discussion over a "revolution in military affairs" with a great deal of emphasis on the technical aspects of that revolution.[92] In short, the general model is that new technological opportunities must be paralleled with organizational and doctrinal development. This model is incomplete, however. When reviewing where doctrine comes from, technology was only one of eleven factors. As navies get more comfortable with the concept of centralized written doctrine, they will have many other opportunities to develop new doctrinal concepts outside of the realm of technology.

Simply put, if doctrine merely follows the push/pull of new technology, then it will miss the opportunity to develop new concepts of operations--and new doctrine--based upon: reviewing newly published policy and strategy; after understanding the latest decisions of resources to be made available to the Services; upon analyses of newly published multinational, joint, multi-Service, other Service, and functional military doctrine and campaign concepts; after another look at actual and emerging threats not foreseen the year before; upon analyses of history and lessons learned; after identifying the strategic culture of newly emerging nations; and upon studying the new geography, demographics, and governments of new nations. All of these non-technology factors could result in new concepts for military doctrine. All of these issues need to be developed by doctrine commands and centers if there is to be a true doctrinal renaissance.

Good military doctrine is of no value without good men and women who are trained and provided the proper equipment. Simply having excellent military doctrine is not enough. History has provided us with examples of navies with superb doctrine but governments that did not support professional military doctrinal development with adequate support for their fighting soldiers, sailors, and airmen. Is this the fault of governments or of the military or both? One should assume that governments will always attempt to minimize their investment in the military, especially in periods of long peace. It is therefore incumbent upon the military to ensure that their needs are explained clearly to governments (who have competing demands) and that the consequences of inattention are expressed in terms of political outputs and not hardware. Doctrine can help professional military officers explain what they do to busy government officials who have a variety of issues other than the military on their plates. Military doctrine reflects a nation's national self-image and self-confidence--and the world watches.

Political leaders will need to ensure that they do not ask too much of their militaries. As long as they include military force as a legitimate tool for the attaining of political objectives, they will bias military doctrine writers toward the offensive. After all, it is with the offensive that a nation makes positive gains. Yet the military professionals need to factor all other inputs to doctrine and make the proper recommendations to their political leadership. Proper recommendations do not include a mindless cheery "aye aye" to all tasking. When all factors influencing doctrine inform the professional that the defensive form of warfare is proper, the senior military leadership must inform their political leadership of the risks involved with the offensive. As experienced in past history, such courage will require an extraordinary officer.

In the absence of continued opportunities to prove the value of combat equipment on an actual battlefield, we will have to turn increasingly to simulations, games, and exercises to attempt to validate doctrinal theories and to help us develop new concepts which will lead to new military doctrine. With the current state of military hardware procurement, it is unrealistic to expect to be able to "fly before you buy" every new weapons system. If we can find substitutes, however, then improvements in hardware may continue in the absence of actual production. At a minimum, such a process could be used in many non-lethal systems.

When good military doctrine is internalized by the training and education afforded to individual soldiers, sailors, marines, and airmen, the results can be seen in success in battle. One observer of the process of war has captured the importance of doctrine and training on shaping the battlefield in terms of describing the preparation of marines for combat on Tarawa during World War II.[93]

> "Marines were the most fearsomely efficient troops on either side in World War II...because Marine recruits were inspired from the beginning with the conviction that they belonged to a select and elite legion...It was the boot-camp training these volunteers endured at Parris Island [South Carolina] that established the foundation of this proud military attitude [which]...spawned in his homesick heart a desperate yearning for order, and finally a love of that order and a clear understanding that in its symmetry lay his safety and survival."

Naval doctrine is not risk free. There are a number of "down sides" to formal naval doctrine. There will always be the natural tension between those who create and want to enforce military doctrine and those who wish to operate at the cutting edges of new ideas. Written naval doctrine presents a target for both intellectual and programmatic change. Rather than fighting over new programs, the first budgetary battles may instead be over the doctrine for their employment. Also, naval doctrine makes one's planned operations more transparent--although in the world of deterrence, this is a partial requirement. Having said all of this, no profession can expect to be allowed to operate as a self-regulating entity without doctrine, and, in this day and age, that doctrine will have to be written.

When military doctrine includes the moral potential of own forces due to *élan*, there is the risk of under-funding for programming and training. Certainly fighting spirit is one of those factors of warfare that is considered in after-action reports. Calculating a warrior spirit as one's military doctrine, however, might again lead to assumptions of short wars and victory by politicians anxious to hold down expenditures.

Perhaps the most risky of all is that of the search for the correct doctrine. With formal doctrine comes "the assumption that there exists a correct and appropriate military doctrine and that, if we only identify it and apply it, we can ensure that military means will serve the chosen aims."[94] There is no one correct and universal military doctrine valid for all time.

No matter how sound the military doctrine, no matter how good the equipment, or how well trained the force, combat is a risky business. Combat requires an evaluation of the situation by a commander and a decision based upon his best overall judgment. Despite the military organization's best efforts to provide the commander with all the tools necessary for sound decision-making, his judgment may, nevertheless, be faulty.

Conclusions

Military doctrine is drawn predominantly, but not totally, from concepts. The inputs to military doctrine include current policy, available resources, current strategy, current doctrine, threats, history and lessons learned, strategic culture, fielded and emerging technology, geography and demographics, and the type of government. Although military doctrine does normally not come from current campaign concepts, the entry into the doctrinal field by the U.S. Navy necessitates inputs from existing doctrine, which means an input from current campaign concepts.

Military doctrine affects how we fight, train, exercise, organize, what we buy, and how we plan. Doctrine for the U.S. Navy does not include tactics, yet tactics, techniques, and procedures (TTP) are directly influenced by doctrine as are local tactical directives. Rules of engagement (ROE) are not derived from doctrine but are affected by it. Training and education go hand in hand with doctrine and cannot be separated from it. Doctrine affects organization, analyses, and campaign planning. By having an impact on campaign planning, military and naval doctrine will affect strategy and, ultimately, policy.

For example, we need to be asking if the military, and especially the naval, doctrine demonstrated successfully during our recent Operations DESERT SHIELD and DESERT STORM is the right military doctrine for tomorrow? Or, is our military thinking still caught up in a Cold War mentality where the enemy is a foreign government (vice a non-governmental actor with military capability) and we need to project forces (instead of the infrastructure)?[95] Is it possible to predict the doctrine that we will need for the future? How do you develop military doctrine in the absence of fielded forces (we did this for the Strategic Defense Initiative - SDI)?

Today, we are witnessing changes in technology as well as the international security environment which will change how navies operate. We are also witnessing a major redirection in government priorities away from the military. The uses of naval forces will change in the future, which will, in turn, require different types of hardware for the fleet. The operating environment may include less public understanding of what we are doing at sea, or with the military in general, and there may be less support for that effort. Under austere fiscal conditions, we may need the military doctrine first to justify why we want to buy various types of weapons systems. Naval doctrine can help us with all of these problems.

Even if we simply focus our initial doctrinal development on current capabilities, before we move on to more advanced concepts of warfare, the shift from open-ocean navy operations to joint littoral warfare will be as traumatic to Western navies as was the shift from the battleship to the aircraft carrier. ...*From the Sea* and the move within the U.S. armed forces to jointness are not business as usual--these are significant and major changes for the Navy. Despite early emphasis on not being perceived as a "revolutionary" organization, the Naval Doctrine Command (NDC) cannot help but be perceived as such.[96] In short, the first order of business for NDC will be to deliver to the fleet naval doctrine that is viewed as "useful."

NDC should first document the naval doctrine of today with the obvious necessity to adjust from open-ocean operations to the joint littoral. Once that is done--no easy task--the next step should be to successfully internalize that doctrine within the fleet. Once the U.S. Navy demonstrates that it accepts formal written doctrine and that it has value, it will then be time to move into the development of doctrine for the future and the inevitable *entree* into the world of programming.

In general, joint, multi-Service, and multinational military doctrine affect the strategic and operational-levels of warfare. In general, Service and functional doctrine affect the tactical-level of warfare. All types of military doctrine are important at the operational-level of warfare. If this is true, doctrinal training and education for officers can be varied by rank with an ever-widening from the combat arms to the multinational or joint perspective. Doctrinal training and education should be associated with leadership training and education. After all, it is the skilled combat leader that must know when to follow doctrine, or when the conditions are so different that deviation is not only authorized but required.

There are some specific differences in how the U.S. Navy and other Services think and are acting about military doctrine. Naval doctrine is a multi-Service doctrine that will be authoritative over but not directive on the U.S. Navy and Marine Corps. It will also affect other military Services and nations that hope to operate with the naval Services.

Naval doctrine is a common cultural perspective of how the naval Services think about war and military operations other than war and will act during time of war and military operations other than war. It is a shared way of thinking that is evolving and dynamic while simultaneously attempting to capture that which is enduring. By following naval doctrine, the leader can reduce human variables to a minimum and remain focused on the mission and not be sidetracked by immediate tasks.

Naval doctrine is composed of those fundamental principles of naval thought and practice that have been internalized by the officer corps. It includes the experiences of others who have been confronted with similar situations. Multi-Service naval doctrine emphasizes the operational-level of warfare and, although affecting sailors, marines, and airmen at every rank, is more of the province of the admiral and commander than the seaman. Without the doctrinal direction of our admirals and commanders, naval warfare would not succeed. In short, it is the heart of naval warfare.

Notes

1. James J. Tritten, "Naval Perspectives for Military Doctrine Development," NDC Technical Report 3-00-003, Norfolk, VA: Naval Doctrine Command, September 1994.

2. James J. Tritten, "Doctrine and Fleet Tactics in the Royal Navy," NDC Technical Report 3-00-004, Norfolk, VA: Naval Doctrine Command, November 1994; "Navy and Military Doctrine in France," NDC Technical Report 3-00-005, Norfolk, VA: Naval Doctrine Command, October 1994; and "Doctrine in the Spanish Navy," NDC Technical Report 3-00-006, Norfolk, VA: Naval Doctrine Command, November 1994; and Rear Admiral Luigi Donolo, ITN, "The History of Italian Naval Doctrine," unpublished paper, Livorno, Italy: *Istituto di Guerra Marittima L'Ammiraglio*, October 1994

3. Rey de Castilla Don Alfonso X el Sabio, *Título XXIV, De la guerra que se face por la mar* [*Of The War That is Made On the Sea*], Maguncia, SP: His Majesty's Royal Council for the Indies 1610 [original version published in 1270].

4. Rear Admiral S.S. Robison, USN (Ret.), *A History of Naval Tactics From 1530 to 1930*, Annapolis, MD: U.S. Naval Institute, 1942, p. 10-11.

5. I am indebted to Bill Lind for this concept, although used in a different context, during a presentation at the Naval Doctrine Command on March 17, 1994.

6. Very little of a scholarly nature has been written to document U.S. Navy doctrine. One attempt was made by Commander William E. Short, Jr., USN, "The Concept of Doctrine: Of Critical Importance But Frequently Misunderstood," Advanced Research Project, Newport, RI: Naval War College, April 1991, p. 94-123. This project does a better job at discussing doctrine in the other Services. Quite frankly, a good 2 man-year project should be funded to do primary research in the archives to document previous doctrinal development in the U.S. Navy.

7. See: Commander in Chief, U.S. Pacific Fleet, *Current Tactical Orders and Doctrine U.S. Pacific Fleet (PAC-10)*, Cincpac File Pac-32-tk, A7-3/A-16-3/P, Serial -1338, June 10, 1943, Figure 1 and p. v. This particular example of Pacific Fleet doctrine is especially

important because it codified multi-carrier task force operations and updated USF-10 due to combat experience. Given the level of controversy over the decisions of Admiral Raymond A. Spruance, USN at the Battle of the Philippine Sea (June 1944) and Admiral William F. Halsey, USN at the Battle of Leyte Gulf (October 1944), it is interesting to note that apparently no one has looked at USF-10 or PAC-10 to see if the task force commander was supposed to remain behind and safeguard the invasion force (as did Spruance) or chase after the enemy battle fleet (as did Halsey) when operating under this doctrine!

8. The *Atlantic Convoy Instructions* (1941 or 1942) were published by the Royal Navy but accepted as doctrine by the U.S. Navy.

9. Admiral Arleigh Burke, USN, Chief of Naval Operations, *Origins of United States Navy Doctrine*, Washington, DC: U.S. Government Printing Office, 11 April 1960; and Admiral James L. Holloway III, USN, *Planning, Readiness and Employment Doctrine for U.S. Naval Operating Forces*, Prepared by the Chief of Information (OP-007), undated.

10. Woodward C. Vann, *The Battle for Leyte Gulf*, New York, NY: McGraw-Hill Book Co., 1947, p. 175.

11. Leonard D. Ash and Martin Hill, "In Harm's Way," *The Retired Officer Magazine*, 50, no. 10 (October 1994): 42-47.

12. Michael A. Palmer, "Burke and Nelson: Decentralized Style of Command," U.S. Naval Institute *Proceedings* 117, no. 7 (July 1991): 58-59; and a copy of the much longer and fully documented original draft of this article supplied by the author.

13. James J. Tritten, "Introduction of Aircraft Carriers into the Royal Navy: Lessons for the Development of Naval Doctrine," *The Naval Review*, 82, no. 3 (July 1994): 260-267; and Norman Friedman, Thomas C. Hone, and Mark D. Mandeles, "The Introduction of Carrier Aviation into the U.S. Navy and the Royal Navy: Military-Technical Revolutions, Organizations, and the Problem of Decision," draft report prepared for the Director, Net Assessment, Office of the Secretary of Defense, May 12, 1994.

14. Captain Stephen Wentworth Roskill, RN (Ret.), *The Strategy of Sea Power: Its Development and Application*, [based upon the Lees-Knowles Lectures delivered in the University of Cambridge, 1961] London, UK: Collins, 1962, p. 64-65.

15. Rear Admiral Yôichi Hirama, JMSDF (Ret.), "Sun Tzü's Influence on the Japanese Imperial Navy," unpublished paper presented at the 2nd International Symposium on Sun Tzü's Art of War, October 16-19, 1990, Beijing, China; and David C. Evans and Mark R. Peattie, *Kaigun [Navy]: Strategy, Tactics and Technology in the Imperial Japanese Navy, 1887-1941*, August 1994 draft book manuscript, chapter 1.

16. Lieutenant Commander Dudley W. Knox, USN, "The Rôle of Doctrine in Naval Warfare," U.S. Naval Institute *Proceedings*, 41, no. 2 (March-April 1915): 325-354,

reprinted in *Art of War Colloquium*, Carlisle Barracks, PA: U.S. Army War College, November 1983, p. 41-70.

17. Although we normally do not think in terms of navy power in the modern Middle East, there is a body of literature which addresses the use of smaller navy forces in littoral operations. For example, see discussions of the Israeli and Arab navies in: Shai Feldman, "Maritime Power and Naval Arms Control in the Mediterranean: Implications in the Middle East Context," and Abdel Monem Said Aly and Mohamed Kadry, "Naval Arms Control in the Southern Mediterranean: An Arab Perspective," both contained in *Europe and Naval Arms Control in the Gorbachev Era*, ed. by Andreas Fürst, Volker Heise, and Steven E. Miller, New York, NY: Oxford University Press for the Stockholm International Peace Research Institute (SIPRI), 1992, pp. 289-323.

18. To a large degree, these lessons appear to have parallels in doctrine ashore, thus undermining the argument that warfare at sea has been shaped by particular technologies or environmental conditions.

19. Headquarters, Department of the Air Force, *Basic Aerospace Doctrine of the United States Air Force*, Air Force Manual 1-1 [AFM 1-1], Vol. II, Washington, DC: U.S. Government Printing Office, March 1992, p. 26-28; and Joint Chiefs of Staff, *Joint Warfare of the US Armed Forces*, Joint Publication 1, Washington, DC: National Defense University Press, 11 November 1991, p. 21.

20. Karl von Clausewitz, *On War*, O.J. Matthijs Jolles, trans., New York, NY: The Modern Library, 1943.

21. Perhaps it is time to spend less time studying "dead Germans." See: Michael A. Palmer, "If Nelson Spoke German," *Military Review*, 69, no. 1 (January 1989): 98-99.

22. Hans Delbrück, *History of the Art of War, Volume I: Warfare in Antiquity*, Walter J. Renfroe, Jr., trans., Lincoln, NE and London, UK: University of Nebraska Press, 1985 [original German version published in 1920], p. 567-568. Delbrück is also credited with destroying the myth of some of Caesar's victories over "impossible" odds. See for example his discussion of Caesar's defeat of Arvernian Vercingetoriz at Alesia, p. 495-507.

23. This section is largely based upon Captain Timothy T. Lupfer, *The Dynamics of Doctrine: The Changes in German Tactical Doctrine During the First World War*, Washington, DC: U.S. Government Printing Office for the Combat Studies Institute, U.S. Army Command and General Staff College, Fort Leavenworth, KS, July 1981.

24. Lieutenant Colonel Robert Allan Doughty, *The Breaking Point: Sedan and the Fall of France, 1940*, Hamden CT: Archon Books, 1990, p. 30-32, 321-332.

25. Ernest H. Jenkins, *A History of the French Navy: From its Beginnings to the Present Day*, London, UK: MacDonald and Jane's, 1973, p. 344.

26. For example, the excellent compilation of British naval documents recently complied by the Navy Records Society does not index the term doctrine, yet contains doctrinal publications--see John B. Hattendorf, et. al., *British Naval Documents: 1204-1960*, Hants, UK: Scolar Press [for the Navy Records Society], 1993. Similarly, when consulting Russian and Soviet military literature, the term military doctrine referred to the wartime preparation of the country as a whole as well as the methods of waging war. Soviet military doctrine fell between military policy and military art and strategy, having both political and military-technical aspects. Chinese military doctrine is similarly placed. See Alexander Chieh-cheng Huang, "The Chinese Navy's Offshore Active Defense Strategy: Conceptualization and Implications," *Naval War College Review*, 47, no. 3 (Summer 1994): 11. In his excellent study of Soviet military doctrine, Ray Garthoff notes that no comprehensive study of "Western military doctrine" exists. See Raymond L. Garthoff, *Soviet Military Doctrine*, Glencoe, IL: The Free Press, 1953, p. 1. By 1984, such studies of Western "military doctrine" existed, but again focused upon more high-level policy issues in addition to how forces fought in the field. For example, see Barry R. Posen, *The Sources of Military Doctrine: France, Britain, and Germany Between the World Wars*, Ithaca, NY: Cornell University Press, 1984. There still has not been any comprehensive study of navy doctrine published in the English-language.

27. Lieutenant Commander Dudley W. Knox, USN, "The Rôle of Doctrine in Naval Warfare," U.S. Naval Institute *Proceedings*, 41, no. 2 (March-April 1915): 341.

28. I am indebted for this point to Major General I[rving]. B[rinton]. Holley, Jr., USAFR (Ret.), during his lecture, "Doctrine: The What, the Why, and the How," given at the Air Force Doctrine Center, Langley AFB, VA, June 1, 1994.

29. The "band of brothers" refers to Admiral Lord Horatio Nelson's captains who fought with him through the Battle of the Nile (1798), although the term is often mis-applied to all of his subordinates, including those at Trafalgar (1805).

30. Admiral Jeremy M. Boorda, USN, "People and Technology: Interview with Chief of Naval Operations Adm. [Admiral] Jeremy M. Boorda" [by Vincent C. Thomas], *Sea Power*, 37, no. 10 (October 1994): 14.

31. E.B. Potter and Fleet Admiral Chester W. Nimitz, USN, eds., *Sea Power: A Naval History*, Englewood Cliffs, NJ: Prentice-Hall, Inc., 1960, p. 366-377; Joseph G. Dawson III, "William T. Sampson and Santiago: Blockade, Victory, and Controversy," *Crucible of Empire: The Spanish-American War & its Aftermath*, Annapolis, MD: Naval Institute Press, 1993, p. 54-55, 60-62; Harold D. Langley, "Winfield S. Schley and Santiago: A New Look at an Old Controversy," *Crucible of Empire: The Spanish-American War & its Aftermath*, Annapolis, MD: Naval Institute Press, 1993, p. 80-81; and Graham A. Cosmas, "Joint Operations in the Spanish-American War," *Crucible of Empire: The Spanish-American War & its Aftermath*, Annapolis, MD: Naval Institute Press, 1993, p. 108-110.

32. Colonel David Jablonsky, USA (Ret.), "US Military Doctrine and the Revolution in Military Affairs," *Parameters*, 24, no. 3 (Autumn 1994): 33.

33. Admiral Jacques Lanxada, FN, Chief of the French Defense Staff, "French Defence Policy After the White Paper," *The RUSI [Royal United Services Institute for Defence Studies] Journal*, 139, no. 2 (April 1994): 19-20.

34. Les Aspin, Secretary of Defense, *Report of the Bottom-Up Review*, Washington, DC: U.S. Government Printing Office, October 1993; and *Annual Report to the President and the Congress*, Washington, DC: U.S. Government Printing Office, January 1994.

35. Captain Richard S. Moore, USMC, "Ideas and Directions: Building Amphibious Doctrine," *Marine Corps Gazette*, 66, no. 11 (November 1982): 58.

36. Dr. Ikuhiko Hata, "A Quantitative Analysis of World War II in the Pacific: Focusing on Naval Air Warfare," presented at the World War II in the Pacific Conference, Alexandria, VA, August 11, 1994.

37. The current head of TRADOC recently emphasized that Army doctrine is not prescriptive. The complexities of attempting to deal with the uncertain future appear to make the U.S. Army less willing to state that their current doctrine is anything more than "as 'nearly right' as it can be." See: General Frederick M. Franks, Jr., USA, "Army Doctrine and the New Strategic Environment," *Ethnic Conflict and Regional Instability: Implications for U.S. Policy and Army Roles and Missions*, Robert L. Pfaltzgraff, Jr. and Richard H. Shultz, Jr., eds., Washington, DC: U.S. Government Printing Office for the U.S. Army War College Strategic Studies Institute, 1994, p. 275-280. Similarly, is a response to an article in the U.S. Naval Institute *Proceedings*, the Commander of the Naval Doctrine Command made the same point that naval doctrine is not prescriptive nor directive. See Rear Admiral Frederick Lewis, USN, "Is There a Doctrine in the House?" [Comment and Discussion], U.S. Naval Institute *Proceedings*, 120, no. 6 (June 1994): 24.

38. Mary H. McCaulley, "The Myers-Briggs Type Indicator and Leadership," *Measures of Leadership*, Kenneth E. Clark & Miriam B. Clark, eds., West Orange, NJ: Leadership Library of America, Inc., for the Center for Creative Leadership, 1990, p. 404, 405, 408, documenting the "tough-minded TJ." The pattern exhibited by most active duty colonel/Navy captains is that of an "ESTJ," or someone who is more extroverted (E) rather than introverted (I), more sensing (S) rather than intuitive (N), more thinking (T) rather than feeling (F), and more judging (J) rather than perceiving (P). The "TJ" pattern would make them less likely to be receptive to new and controversial ideas.

39. The similarity between military doctrine and religious doctrine has been noted in the past. For example, the new Director General of Land Warfare in Great Britain noted that "the only reason that I got my job was because I was a Catholic and only Catholics understand doctrine." See Major General M.A. Willcocks, *The RUSI [Royal United Services Institute for Defence Studies] Journal*, 139, no. 3 (June 1994): 6.

40. David C. Evans and Mark R. Peattie, *Kaigun [Navy]: Strategy, Tactics and Technology in the Imperial Japanese Navy, 1887-1941*, August 1994 draft book manuscript, chapter 1.

41. Hans Delbrück, *History of the Art of War, Volume IV: The Dawn of Modern Warfare*, Walter J. Renfroe, Jr., trans., Lincoln, NE and London, UK: University of Nebraska Press, 1985 [original German version published in 1920], p. 390, 398, 402, 414.

42. Hans Delbrück, *History of the Art of War, Volume III: Medieval Warfare*, Walter J. Renfroe, Jr., trans., Lincoln, NE and London, UK: University of Nebraska Press, 1985 [original German version published in 1923], p. 468, 635; and *History of the Art of War, Volume IV: The Dawn of Modern Warfare*, Walter J. Renfroe, Jr., trans., Lincoln, NE and London, UK: University of Nebraska Press, 1985 [original German version published in 1920], p. 41, 126.

43. Hans Delbrück, *History of the Art of War, Volume III: Medieval Warfare*, Walter J. Renfroe, Jr., trans., Lincoln, NE and London, UK: University of Nebraska Press, 1985 [original German version published in 1923], p. 635, 650.

44. Japanese amphibious warfare doctrine developed in parallel with that of the U.S. Marine Corps. The Japanese Army was in a different position vis-a-vis the Navy than in the United States and was able to secure earlier cooperation in the development of landing craft. The *Shinshu Maru*, the world's first ship specifically designed for amphibious operations--a prototype for what would later become the landing ship dock--was laid down in 1933 and completed in 1934--years before anything similar in the U.S. See David C. Evans and Mark R. Peattie, *Kaigun [Navy]: Strategy, Tactics and Technology in the Imperial Japanese Navy, 1887-1941*, August 1994 draft book manuscript, chapter 14.

45. David C. Evans and Mark R. Peattie, *Kaigun [Navy]: Strategy, Tactics and Technology in the Imperial Japanese Navy, 1887-1941*, August 1994 draft book manuscript, chapter 8.

46. Commander Charles M. Melhorn, USN (Ret.), *Two-Block Fox: The Rise of the Aircraft Carrier, 1911-1929*, Annapolis, MD: Naval Institute Press, 1974, 181 pp.

47. Dr. Dean Allard, "The U.S. Navy Prepares for War," unpublished paper presented at the World War II in the Pacific Conference, Alexandria, VA, August 10, 1994, p. 8.

48. I am indebted to Dr. James R. Reckner, Texas Tech University, for having provided me information on U.S. naval doctrine at the turn of the century. Dr. Reckner has done primary research using the Naval War College Archives, the General Board Letterbooks, and the Moody Papers in the Library of Congress. He will fully develop these materials in a forthcoming book tentatively entitled *The United States Navy in the Era of Theodore Roosevelt*, to be published by the Naval Historical Center.

49. Captain Timothy T. Lupfer, USA, *The Dynamics of Doctrine: The Changes in German Tactical Doctrine During the First World War*, Washington, DC: U.S. Government Printing

Office for the Combat Studies Institute, U.S. Army Command and General Staff College, Fort Leavenworth, KS, July 1981.

50. Paul S. Dull, *A Battle History of the Imperial Japanese Navy (1941-1945)*, Annapolis, MD, Naval Institute Press, 1978, p. 35-41.

51. Geoffrey Till, *Air Power and the Royal Navy 1914-1945: A Historical Survey*, London, UK: Jane's Publishing Co., 1979, p. 149.

52. Stephen Peter Rosen, *Winning the Next War: Innovation and the Modern Military*, Ithaca, NY and London, UK: Cornell University Press, 1991.

53. Harold R. Winton, *To Change an Army: General Sir John Burnett-Stuart and British Armored Doctrine, 1927-1938*, Lawrence, KS: University Press of Kansas, 1988, p. 240.

54. John D. Harbron, *Trafalgar and the Spanish Navy*, Washington, DC: Naval Institute Press, 1988, p. 98-102.

55. David C. Evans and Mark R. Peattie, *Kaigun [Navy]: Strategy, Tactics and Technology in the Imperial Japanese Navy, 1887-1941*, August 1994 draft book manuscript, chapters 2 & 3.

56. Department of the Navy, *...From the Sea: Preparing the Naval Service for the 21st Century*, Washington, D.C., September 1992.

57. Department of the Navy, *Forward...From the Sea*, Washington, D.C., September 1994.

58. Norman Friedman, Thomas C. Hone, and Mark D. Mandeles, "The Introduction of Carrier Aviation into the U.S. Navy and the Royal Navy: Military-Technical Revolutions, Organizations, and the Problem of Decision," draft report prepared for the Director, Net Assessment, Office of the Secretary of Defense, May 12, 1994, p. 207.

59. This opinion is also shared by Major General I[rving]. B[rinton]. Holley, Jr., USAFR, "The Doctrinal Process: Some Suggested Steps," *Military Review*, 59, no. 4 (April 1979): 3.

60. Admiral Jeremy M. Boorda, USN, "People and Technology: Interview with Chief of Naval Operations Adm. [Admiral] Jeremy M. Boorda" [by Vincent C. Thomas], *Sea Power*, 37, no. 10 (October 1994): 14-15 uses the "playbook" analogy.

61. General Maxwell Thurman, USA, presentation contained in the *Strategic Leadership Conference: Proceedings*, Carlisle Barracks, PA and Alexandria, VA: U.S. Army War College and the U.S. Army Research Institute, February 1991, p. 25, 31.

62. Stephen Peter Rosen, *Winning the Next War: Innovation and the Modern Military*, Ithaca, NY and London, UK: Cornell University Press, 1991, p. 70, 82-85.

63. Major General I[rving]. B[rinton]. Holley, Jr., USAFR, "The Doctrinal Process: Some Suggested Steps," *Military Review*, 59, no. 4 (April 1979): 2-13.

64. James J. Tritten "Is Naval Warfare Unique?" *The Journal of Strategic Studies*, 12, no. 4 (December 1989): 494-507.

65. Hans Delbrück, *History of the Art of War, Volume II: The Barbarian Invasions*, Walter J. Renfroe, Jr., trans., Lincoln, NE and London, UK: University of Nebraska Press, 1985 [original German version published in 1921], p. 411, and *History of the Art of War, Volume III: Medieval Warfare*, Walter J. Renfroe, Jr., trans., Lincoln, NE and London, UK: University of Nebraska Press, 1985 [original German version published in 1923], p. 327.

66. A good place to start might be the extremely well-developed case study of the difficulty in changing British Army armored doctrine, see: Harold R. Winton, *To Change an Army: General Sir John Burnett-Stuart and British Armored Doctrine, 1927-1938*, Lawrence, KS: University Press of Kansas, 1988. Further development of the British Army case study might lead to the discovery of contrasting doctrinal climates as can be seen in the French case.

67. This point is made, in a slightly different context, in John M. Collins, *Military Preparedness: Principles Compared With U.S. Practices*, CRS 94-48 S, Washington, DC: Congressional Research Service, January 21, 1994, p. 42.

68. A. Savelyev, vice president of the Institute of National Security and Strategic Studies, "Does Russia Need a 'Potential Enemy'?" Moscow *Krasnaya Zvezda* in Russian, March 19, 1992, p. 2 (FBIS-SOV-92-100, May 22, 1992, pp. 33-35).

69. Gideon Y. Akavia, "Defensive Defense and the Nature of Armed Conflict," *The Journal of Strategic Studies*, 14, no. 1 (March 1991): 27-48; and *Decisive Victory and Correct Doctrine: Cults in French Military Thought Before 1914*, Stanford, CA: Center for International Security and Arms Control, Stanford University, November 1993.

70. David C. Evans and Mark R. Peattie, *Kaigun [Navy]: Strategy, Tactics and Technology in the Imperial Japanese Navy, 1887-1941*, August 1994 draft book manuscript. In part, the over-emphasis on the offensive can be attributed to the naval doctrinal renaissance in Japan occurring about the same time as the writings of Rear Admiral Alfred Thayer Mahan, USN and the assignment of British Navy officers to teach in Japan.

71. For an extremely thought-provoking discourse on the relationship between offensive and defensive warfare and the anti-effeminate bias of military officers, see: Norman Dixon, *On the Psychology of Military Incompetence*, New York, NY: Basic Books, Inc., 1976, p. 208-213.

72. Sun Tzu, *The Art of War*, Brigader General Samuel B. Griffith, USMC (Ret.), trans., New York, NY: Oxford University Press, 1963.

73. Headquarters, United States Marine Corps, *Warfighting*, FMFM [Fleet Marine Force Manual] 1, Washington, DC: 6 March 1989, p. 17.

74. *The Seven Military Classics of Ancient China*, Ralph D. Sawyer, trans., Boulder, CO: Westview Press, 1993 contains additional texts that set Sun Tzu's *The Art of War* into a more coherent whole.

75. Lao Tzu, *Tao Te Ching (The Book of the Way)*, Stephen Mitchell, trans. and ed., New York, NY: Harper Collins Publishers, 1988, p. 69.

76. Rear Admiral Yôichi Hirama, JMSDF (Ret.), "Sun Tzü's Influence on the Japanese Imperial Navy," unpublished paper presented at the 2nd International Symposium on Sun Tzü's Art of War, October 16-19, 1990, Beijing, China.

77. In Barry R. Posen, *The Sources of Military Doctrine: France, Britain, and Germany Between the World Wars*, Ithaca, NY: Cornell University Press, 1984, military doctrine is cast as being offensive, defensive, or deterrent. Although my own studies do not use this paradigm, Posen's work on the offensive vs. the defensive have merit for naval audiences.

78. Gunther E. Rothenberg, "Maurice of Nassau, Gustavus Adolphus, Raimondo Montecuccoli, and the 'Military Revolution' of the Seventeenth Century," *Makers of Modern Strategy: From Machiavelli to the Nuclear Age*, ed. Peter Paret, Princeton, NJ: Princeton University Press, 1986, p. 55-57.

79. Gunther E. Rothenberg, "Moltke, Schlieffen, and the Doctrine of Strategic Envelopment," *Makers of Modern Strategy: From Machiavelli to the Nuclear Age*, ed. Peter Paret, Princeton, NJ: Princeton University Press, 1986, p. 296; David H. Zook, Jr. and Robin Higham, *A Short History of Warfare*, New York, NY: Twayne Publishers, 1966, p. 238.

80. Gordon A. Craig, "Delbrück: The Military Historian," *Makers of Modern Strategy: From Machiavelli to the Nuclear Age*, ed. Peter Paret, Princeton, NJ: Princeton University Press, 1986, p. 341-342; and Michael Geyer, "German Strategy in the Age of Machine Warfare, 1914-1945," *Makers of Modern Strategy: From Machiavelli to the Nuclear Age*, ed. Peter Paret, Princeton, NJ: Princeton University Press, 1986, p. 531.

81. Condoleezza Rice, "The Making of Soviet Strategy," *Makers of Modern Strategy: From Machiavelli to the Nuclear Age*, ed. Peter Paret, Princeton, NJ: Princeton University Press, 1986, p. 665, 673.

82. Aleksandr A. Svechin, *Strategy*, ed. Kent D. Lee, Minneapolis, MN: East View Publications, 1992 [translation of 1927 original Russian-language edition], p. 239-250.

83. Toshikazu Ohmae, "The Battle of Savo Island," and associated comment by Admiral

Mikawa Gun'ichi, *The Japanese Navy in World War II: In the Words of Former Japanese Naval Officers*, 2nd ed., Annapolis, MD: Naval Institute Press, 1986, p. 242, 244.

84. Hans Delbrück, *History of the Art of War, Volume IV: The Dawn of Modern Warfare*, Walter J. Renfroe, Jr., trans., Lincoln, NE and London, UK: University of Nebraska Press, 1985 [original German version published in 1920], p. 335-337.

85. Karl von Clausewitz, *On War*, O.J. Matthijs Jolles, trans., New York, NY: The Modern Library, 1943, p. 209-210.

86. Thomas B. Buell, "Oral Histories Help Tell the Tale," U.S. Naval Institute *Proceedings*, 120, no. 7 (July 1994): 47.

87. Hans Delbrück, *History of the Art of War, Volume IV: The Dawn of Modern Warfare*, Walter J. Renfroe, Jr., trans., Lincoln, NE and London, UK: University of Nebraska Press, 1985 [original German version published in 1920], p. 375, 378-380.

88. Hans Delbrück, *History of the Art of War, Volume IV: The Dawn of Modern Warfare*, Walter J. Renfroe, Jr., trans., Lincoln, NE and London, UK: University of Nebraska Press, 1985 [original German version published in 1920], p. 380 argues that there is no such thing as pure "maneuver" warfare. For an opposing view, see: William S. Lind, *Maneuver Warfare Handbook*, Boulder, CO: Westview Press, 1985; and Richard D. Hooker, Jr., ed., *Maneuver Warfare: An Anthology*, Novato, CA: Presidio Press, 1993.

89. See especially the writings of Admiral Raoul Victor Patrice Castex, FN. His five volume *Théories stratégiques* are perhaps the most complete theoretical survey of maritime strategy to ever appear. A sixth volume, *Mélanges stratégiques*, was published in 1976 after his death. The essence of Castex's work can be found in a summary of some 2,600 pages of original text in French translated into 428 pages in English in *Strategic Theories*, selections translated and edited, with an introduction by Eugenia C. Kiesling, Annapolis, MD: Naval Institute Press, 1994.

90. David C. Evans and Mark R. Peattie, *Kaigun [Navy]: Strategy, Tactics and Technology in the Imperial Japanese Navy, 1887-1941*, August 1994 draft book manuscript, chapter 2.

91. Naval Doctrine Command, *Naval Warfare*, NDP-1, Washington, DC: U.S. Government Printing Office, 28 March 1994.

92. Colonel David Jablonsky, USA (Ret.), "US Military Doctrine and the Revolution in Military Affairs," *Parameters*, 24, no. 3 (Autumn 1994): 18-36.

93. Martin Russ, *Line of Departure: Tarawa*, Garden City, NY: Doubleday & Co., 1975, p. 39-40.

94. Gideon Y. Akavia, *Decisive Victory and Correct Doctrine: Cults in French Military Thought Before 1914*, Stanford, CA: Center for International Security and Arms Control, Stanford University, November 1993, p. 4-5.

95. To stretch your mind, I highly recommend Alvin and Heidi Toffler, *War and Anti-War: Survival at the Dawn of the 21st Century*, Boston, MA: Little, Brown and Co., 1993.

96. The choice of role of the Naval Doctrine Command as being revolutionary or evolutionary has been well explained by Commander Rey Arellano, USN and Richard D. Kohout in "Realizing the New Maritime Strategy Through Doctrine Development," CRM 93-21, Alexandria, VA: Center for Naval Analyses, July 1993, 65 pp.

DISTRIBUTION LIST

Commander (00)   1
Naval Doctrine Command
1540 Gilbert Street
Norfolk, VA 23511-2785

Deputy Commander (01)   1
Naval Doctrine Command
1540 Gilbert Street
Norfolk, VA 23511-2785

Science Advisor (02SA)   1
Naval Doctrine Command
1540 Gilbert Street
Norfolk, VA 23511-2785

Technical and Financial Division (02T)   1
Naval Doctrine Command
1540 Gilbert Street
Norfolk, VA 23511-2785

Center for Naval Analyses Representative (02EG)   1
Naval Doctrine Command
1540 Gilbert Street
Norfolk, VA 23511-2785

Naval Doctrine Development Division (N3)   1
Naval Doctrine Command
1540 Gilbert Street
Norfolk, VA 23511-2785

Joint/Combined Doctrine Division (N5)   1
Naval Doctrine Command
1540 Gilbert Street
Norfolk, VA 23511-2785

Evaluation, Training, and Education Division (N7)   1
Naval Doctrine Command
1540 Gilbert Street
Norfolk, VA 23511-2785

Strategy and Concepts Division (N8)   1
Naval Doctrine Command
1540 Gilbert Street
Norfolk, VA 23511-2785

Health Service Support Division (N9)   1
Naval Doctrine Command
2200 Lester Street
Quantico, VA 22134-6050

Dr. James J. Tritten (N5A) Naval Doctrine Command 1540 Gilbert Street Norfolk, VA 23511-2785	3
Australian Liaison Officer (N5AU) Naval Doctrine Command 1540 Gilbert Street Norfolk, VA 23511-2785	1
British Liaison Officer (N5B) Naval Doctrine Command 1540 Gilbert Street Norfolk, VA 23511-2785	1
Canadian Liaison Officer (N5C) Naval Doctrine Command 1540 Gilbert Street Norfolk, VA 23511-2785	1
French Liaison Officer (N5F) Naval Doctrine Command 1540 Gilbert Street Norfolk, VA 23511-2785	1
Italian Liaison Officer (N5I) Naval Doctrine Command 1540 Gilbert Street Norfolk, VA 23511-2785	1
Library Naval Historical Center Building 57 Washington Navy Yard 901 M Street, S.E. Washington, DC 20374-0571	1
Joint Warfighting Center Attn: Joint Electronic Library (JEL) Building 100, Ingalls Road Fort Monroe, VA 23651-5000	1
Joint Doctrine Division Air Force Doctrine Center 216 Sweeney Blvd., Suite 109 Langley AFB, VA 23665-2792	1
Headquarters Joint Doctrine Division Deputy Chief of Staff for Doctrine Attn: ATDO-J U.S. Army Training and Doctrine Command Fort Monroe, VA 23651	1

Library Center for Naval Analyses 4401 Ford Avenue Alexandria, VA 22302-0268	1
Armed Forces Staff College Attn: LIB/62 7800 Hampton Blvd. Norfolk, VA 23511-1702	1
Defense Technical Information Center Attn: DTIC-OCC Building 5 Cameron Station Alexandria, VA 22304-6145	2
Dr. Gideon Y. Akavia CEMA - Center for Military Analyses P.O. Box 2250 (28) 31021 Haifa, Israel - *via air mail* -	1
Dr. Roger Barnett Joint Operations Division - Code 12 Naval War College 686 Cushing Road Newport, RI 02841-5010	1
Dr. Susan Canedy Office of the Command Historian Attn: ATMH U.S. Army Training and Doctrine Command Fort Monroe, VA 23651	1
COL John Collins, USA (Ret.) Congressional Research Service Library of Congress, LM-315 Madison Building 1st and Independence Avenues, S.E. Washington, DC 20540	1
CAPT George Conner, USN Code OR/Co Department of Operations Research Naval Postgraduate School Monterey, CA 93943-5100	1
Mr. Hervé Coutau-Bégarie *Commission Francaise d'Histoire Maritime* *Archives Nationales* 60 rue des Franc-Bourgeois 75144 Paris CEDEX 03, France - *via air mail* -	1

CAPT Alain Delbury, FN   1
French Military Mission to SACLANT
7857 Blandy Road, Suite 100
Norfolk, VA 23551-2490

CAPT Hughes de Longevialle, FN   1
French Naval Attaché
Embassy of France
4101 Reservoir Rd., NW
Washington, DC 20007-2171

RADM J.L. Duval, FN   1
Centre d'Enseignement Superieur de la Marine
21 Place Joffre
75700 Paris, France - *via air mail* -

CAPT Theodore Ferriter, USN   1
Air-Land-Sea Applications (ALSA) Center
114 Andrews Street, Suite 101
Langley AFB, VA 23665-2785

CAPT Thom Ford, USN   1
Attn: ATZL-SWL-N
U.S. Army Command and General Staff College
Fort Leavenworth, KS 66027-5015

Rear Admiral José Ignacio González-Aller Hierro, SPN   1
Director
Museo Naval de Madrid
Paseo del Prado, 5
28071 Madrid, España - *via air mail* -

CAPT Jaime Goyeness, SPN   1
Spanish Military Mission to SACLANT
7857 Blandy Road, Suite 100
Norfolk, VA 23551-2490

Dr. Thomas Grassey   1
Editor, *Naval War College Review* - Code 32
Naval War College
686 Cushing Road
Newport, RI 02841-1207

Eric J. Grove   1
Department of Politics
Centre for Security Studies
The University of Hull
Hull HU6 7RX United Kingdom - *via air mail* -

Dr. John Hattendorf   1
Director, Advanced Research Department - Code 35
Naval War College
686 Cushing Road
Newport, RI 02841-1207

LTG I.B. Holley, USAFR (Ret.)   1
Professor Emeritus
Department of History
226 Carr Building - East Campus
Duke University
P.O. Box 90719
Durham, NC 27708-0719

CAPT Wayne Hughes, USN (Ret.)   1
Code OR/H1
Department of Operations Research
Naval Postgraduate School
Monterey, CA 93943-5100

Dr. John H. Johns   1
Dean of Faculty and Programs
Industrial College of the Armed Forces, Room 228
Fort Leslie J. McNair
Washington, DC 20319-6000

Professor Kevin Kelly   1
National Strategy Decisionmaking Department - Code 1B
Naval War College
686 Cushing Road
Newport, RI 02841-1207

Commander Joe Kidd, RN   1
Directorate Naval Staff Duties
Room 6386, Main Building
Ministry of Defence, Whitehall
London SW1A 2MB - *via air mail* -

Professor Eugenia Kiesling   1
Department of History
University of Alabama
Box 870212
Tuscaloosa, AL 35487-0212

Commander Alfredo Maglietta, ITN   1
Administrative Assistant to the Commander
Italian Naval War College
Livorno, Italy - *via air mail* -

Dr. Edward J. Marolda   1
Head, Contemporary History Branch
Naval Historical Center
Building 57
Washington Navy Yard
901 M Street, S.E.
Washington, DC 20374-0571

Andrew Marshall   1
OSD/NA, Pentagon Room 3A930
Director, Net Assessment
Office of the Secretary of Defense
Washington, DC 20301

Professeur Philippe Masson   1
Chef de la Section Travaux Historiques
    Service Historique de la Marine
Pavillion de la Reine
Château de Vincennes
B.P. N° 2
00300 Amée, France - *via air mail* -

CAPT Jack McCaffrie, RAN   1
Director General, Maritime Studies Program
ANZAC Park West
APW2-G-11
Department of Defence
Canberra ACT 2600 Australia - *via air mail* -

CAPT Ryan McCombie, USN   1
ATTN: USAWC/AWC-J
Army War College
Carlisle Barracks, PA 17013-5050

LTC Dave Mirra, USMC   1
Doctrine Division - C42
Marine Corps Combat Development Command (MCCDC)
2042 Broadway, Suite 205
Quantico, VA 22134-5021

Dr. James A. Mowbray   1
Code AWC/DFX
Air War College
Maxwell AFB, AL 36112-6427

CAPT Christopher Nelson, USN (Ret.)   1
TACTRAGRULANT
2132 Regulus Avenue
FCTCLANT Dam Neck
Virginia Beach, VA 23461-5596

CAPT Michael F. O'Brien, USN   1
Code: NDU-INSS-ROSA
Institute for National Strategic Studies, Room 314
National Defense University
Fort Leslie J. McNair
Washington, DC 20319-6000

Professor Paul Odell   1
Strategy Department - Code 1A
Naval War College
686 Cushing Road
Newport, RI 02841-1207

CAPT Chris Page, RN   1
Head of Defence Studies (RN)
Room 5391 Main Building
Ministry of Defence - Whitehall
London SW1A 2HB United Kingdom - *via air mail* -

CAPT John N. Petrie, USN   1
Director of Writing & Research
Code: NWC-NWFA
National War College
Ft. Leslie J. McNair
Washington, DC 20319-6000

Dr. Bruce Powers   1
N-88W, Pentagon Room 4E367
Office of the Chief of Naval Operations
Washington, DC 20350-2000

COL Jon Stull, USMC   1
Code DDCD
Armed Forces Staff College
7800 Hampton Blvd.
Norfolk, VA 23511-1702

CAPT Peter Swartz, USN (Ret.)   1
Center for Naval Analyses (CNA)
4401 Ford Avenue
Alexandria, VA 22302-0268

LTC John Taxeras, USMC   1
Attn: Code C40OP2
Marine Corps University
Marine Corps Combat Development Command (MCCDC)
2076 South Street
Quantico, VA 22134-5021

Dr. Geoffrey Till   1
Department of History and International Affairs
King Williams Walk
Royal Naval College Greenwich
London SE10 9NN United Kingdom - *via air mail* -

Dr. Milan Vego   1
Department of Operations
686 Cushing Road
Naval War College
Newport, RI 02841-5010

CDR Michael Vitale, USN   1
Joint Doctrine Division
The Pentagon, Room 1A724
Washington, DC 20318-7000

CAPT George Wilson, USN   1
Code: AU/CCN
Air War College
325 Chennault Circle
Maxwell AFB, AL 36112-6427

www.ingramcontent.com/pod-product-compliance
Lightning Source LLC
Chambersburg PA
CBHW080602090426
42735CB00016B/3318